INCORPORATION AND BUSINESS GUIDE FOR ONTARIO

INCORPORATION AND BUSINESS GUIDE FOR ONTARIO

M. Stephen Georgas, LLB

Self-Counsel Press
(a division of)
International Self-Counsel Press Ltd.
Canada   USA

Self-Counsel Press acknowledges the financial support of the Government of Canada through the Book Publishing Industry Development Program (BPIDP) for our publishing activities.

Printed in Canada.

First edition: 1972
Tenth edition: 1989
Fifteenth edition: 1996; Reprinted: 1997
Sixteenth edition: 1998; Reprinted 1999
Seventeenth edition: 2000; Reprinted 2002
Eighteenth edition: 2003

National Library of Canada Cataloguing in Publication

Georgas, M. Stephen, 1949-
    Incorporation and business guide for Ontario: how to form your own corporation/M. Stephen Georgas.—18th ed.

    (Self-counsel legal series)
    ISBN 1-55180-561-8

    1. Incorporation—Ontario—Popular works. I. Title. II. Series.
KEO403.Z82G46 2003   346.713'06622   C2003-905453-5

GEO

Self-Counsel Press
(a division of)
International Self-Counsel Press Ltd.

1481 Charlotte Road	1704 N. State Street
North Vancouver, BC V7J lHl	Bellingham, WA 98225
Canada	USA

CONTENTS

TABLES

SAMPLES

NOTICE TO READERS

Laws are constantly changing. Every effort is made to keep this publication as current as possible. However, the author, the publisher, and the vendor of this book make no representation or warranties regarding the outcome or the use to which the information in this book is put and are not assuming any liability for any claims, losses, or damages arising out of the use of this book. The reader should not rely on the author or the publisher of this book for any professional advice. Please be sure that you have the most recent edition.

Note: The fees quoted in this book are correct at the date of publication. However, fees are subject to change without notice. For current fees, please check with the court registry or appropriate government office nearest you.

AVAILABLE FROM THE PUBLISHER

In order to incorporate your business, you will need to file certain forms. You may type these yourself, but it is easier and quicker to use preprinted forms. The practice has grown in the legal profession of using certain standard printed forms that ease the typing load considerably. The prepackaged forms with computer disk are available where you bought this book or you may use the order form on the next page. The cost of each package is $21.95.

The set includes:

2 sets of Articles of Incorporation

2 Consent to Act as First Director forms

1 General By-law

4 share certificates

Also available are the following items:

Company seal — $53.50 (The seal should not be ordered until you have received your Certificate of Incorporation.)

Minute book — $24.95

Deposit stamp — "For deposit only to the credit of (Company name)" — $16.95

Endorsement stamp — "Company Name" — $12.95

Name and address stamp — $16.95

Extra share certificates — 50¢ each

Note: Please allow three to four weeks for delivery. Prices are subject to change without notice.

ORDER FORM

Clip out page and send or fax to: **Self-Counsel Press, 4 Bram Court,**
Brampton, ON L6W 3R6
Telephone: 1-800-387-3362 Fax: (905) 450-7626

Please send the following items prepaid:

QUANTITY		PRICE PER UNIT	TOTAL
_____	Package form & disk kit	$21.95	$ _____
_____	Seal	53.50	_____
_____	Minute book	24.95	_____
_____	Deposit stamp (with two lines)	16.95	_____
_____	Endorsement stamp	12.95	_____
_____	Name and address stamp	16.95	_____
_____	Extra share certificates	0.50	_____
	Subtotal		$ _____
	8% PST on subtotal amount		_____
	7% GST on subtotal amount		_____
	Postage and handling (includes GST)	5.00	_____
	Postage and handling for rush orders (includes GST)	10.00	_____
	TOTAL		$ _____

❑ Money order enclosed

❑ Please charge the TOTAL amount to my   ❑ Visa   ❑ MasterCard.
    I have filled in the information indicated below and signed where requested.

Please send the items checked above to:

Mr./Ms.: _____

Address: _____

City: _____ Province: _____

Postal code: _____ Telephone: _____

Name of corporation: _____
_____

Corporation address (for stamp) if not same as above: _____

Visa/MasterCard Number: _____

Validation date: _____ Expiry date: _____

Signature: _____

Please check your seals and stamps upon receipt. We are not responsible for errors reported more than 30 days after mailing. Prices are subject to change without notice.

❑ **Check here for a free catalogue of all Self-Counsel's books.**

PREFACE

The purpose of this book is to provide sufficient information of a legal and practical nature to assist you in understanding incorporation procedures and to enable you to incorporate your own corporation.

By following the procedures set out in this book, you can save a substantial amount in legal fees for incorporating a corporation.

The book applies to a corporation that does not offer its securities to the public — in other words, the "private corporation."

By explaining each step of an actual incorporation, the book will not only enable you to incorporate your own corporation, but will also provide information to help you maintain your corporate status. Once your corporation is incorporated, you must attend to various matters on a continual basis to preserve that status.

If questions of a complicated nature arise, such as tax, estate planning, shareholders' agreements, or basic structural corporate changes, you should seek competent legal and accounting advice.

In any case, it is recommended that competent professional help be sought as your business grows and with it your need for legal, accounting, financial, and other advice. This book is not meant to circumvent or to derogate from the value of professional help. It is meant as an aid to people who desire to incorporate and who simply want to become acquainted with the legal and practical implications of incorporation.

The incorporation procedures set out in the book apply only to "profit-making" businesses, not clubs, social corporations, co-operatives, credit unions, or the like.

The act governing the incorporation of businesses is administered by the Ministry of Consumer and Business Services, Companies and Personal Property Security Branch (CPPSB), whose members have been most co-operative and helpful in providing valuable assistance.

ACKNOWLEDGMENTS

I would like to express my gratitude to Paul Edmonds and Gerry Courage, lawyers with the law firm Miller Thomson, LLP, for their assistance in editing chapter 2, and to Brenda Taylor and Sherry Provis, corporate law clerks with Miller Thomson, LLP, for editing this edition of the *Guide*.

1

INTRODUCTION TO THE INCORPORATED BUSINESS

You are probably already engaged in a small business or are thinking about starting one up, either by yourself or with someone else. One of the first decisions to be made in dealing with the question of starting a business is whether your business "vehicle" should be a proprietorship, partnership (two or more persons), or a limited corporation.

a. METHODS OF CARRYING ON BUSINESS

Whether you run a small corner grocery store or a large business like General Motors of Canada Limited, there are only three ways to carry on any business: through a corporation, as a sole proprietor, or as a partner in a business. There are also special entities in existence, such as organizations engaged in charitable or semi-charitable enterprises. These do not concern us here and will not be discussed.

1. The sole proprietorship and partnership

You are free to carry on business under practically any name you or your partners choose, subject to a possible "passing off" action for appropriating someone else's name or to a trademark infringement action. It is important to realize, however, that the law does not recognize the name of a proprietorship or partnership and, in any legal action, the proprietor and/or partners must be named personally.

For example, Joe Citizen, carrying on business as XYZ GROCERY, if sued, would be named as "JOE CITIZEN carrying on business under the firm name and style of XYZ GROCERY." The legal consequences of carrying on business in this fashion are explained later on.

The assets of a proprietorship belong to the individual parties and not to the business. Further, parties carrying on business either as a proprietorship or partnership are personally liable for any debts they incur through the business in favor of third-party creditors.

In addition, partners are fully liable for debts incurred by each other while acting in the course of business. That is, they are jointly and severally liable, regardless of the proportionate capital contribution of the individual parties.

It is important to realize that you may be deemed to be in partnership with someone even though you have made no formal declaration of such a partnership. (See Sample 1 for an example of a formal declaration.) This is because a partnership is created by the relationship of the parties and not by any formal act or documents signed by the parties.

You can register a proprietorship or partnership pursuant to the Business Names Act (Ontario) with the Minister of Consumer and Business Services by completing a registration form available from the Companies and Personal Property Security Branch (CPPSB) and paying $80. (Electronic filing is also available.)

There is no established test as to what constitutes a partnership, although the following questions are a guide.

1

SAMPLE 1
BUSINESS NAME REGISTRATION FORM

Ontario

Ministry of Consumer and Business Services

Ministère des Services aux consommateurs et aux entreprises

Registration Form 1
under the Business Names Act - Sole Proprietorship / Partnership
Enregistrement Formule 1
en vertu de la *Loi sur les noms commerciaux*
(Entreprise personnelle / société en nom collectif)

Print clearly in CAPITAL LETTERS /
Écrivez clairement en LETTRES MAJUSCULES

1. Registration Type / Type d'enregistrement

If B, C, or D enter "Business Identification Number" /
En cas de B, C ou D, inscrivez le n° d'identification de l'entreprise.

Page _____ of / de _____

A ☒ New / Nouvel   B ☐ Renewal / Renouvellement   C ☐ Amendment / Modification   D ☐ Cancellation / Révocation   BIN Business Identification No./ NIE le n° d'identification de l'entreprise

2. Business Name / Nom commercial

J & J INDUSTRIES

3. Mailing Address / Adresse postale

Street No./ N° de rue   Street Name / Nom de la rue   Suite No. / Bureau n°
1720 EGLINGTON AVENUE EAST

City / Town / Ville   Province / Province   Postal Code / Code postal
TORONTO   ONTARIO   Z1P 0G0

Country / Pays
CANADA

4. Address of principal place of business in Ontario (P.O. Box not acceptable) /
Adresse de l'établissement principal en Ontario *(Case postale non acceptée)*

☐ Same as above / comme ci-dessus

Street No./ N° de rue   Street Name / Nom de la rue   Suite No. / Bureau n°   City / Town / Ville

Province / Province   Country / Pays   Postal Code / Code postal
ONTARIO   CANADA

5. Give a brief description of the ACTIVITY being carried out under the business name./
Résumez brièvement le genre d'ACTIVITÉ exercée sous le nom commercial.

ANTIQUE BOTTLE SALES

6. Type of Registrant / Type de personne enregistrée

A ☐ Sole proprietorship / Entreprise personnelle   B ☒ Partnership / Société en nom collectif   ☐ More than 10 Partners: records at business address / Plus de 10 associés : dossiers à l'adresse d'affaires

7. Registrant Information / Renseignements sur la personne enregistrée

Last Name / Nom de famille   First Name / Prénom   Middle Initial / initiale 2e prénom
DOE   JOHN   D.

8. Street No./ N° de rue   Street Name / Nom de la rue   Suite No. / Bureau n°   City / Town / Ville
1200 ORIOLE PARKWAY   SUITE 101 TORONTO

Province / Province   Country / Pays   Postal Code / Code postal
ONTARIO   CANADA   Z1P 0G0

Additional Information. Only complete if the registrant is not an individual. See instructions 7/8 on the form. /
Renseignements supplémentaires. À remplir uniquement si la personne enregistrée n'est pas un particulier.
Voir les instructions 7 et 8 sur le formulaire.

Ont. Corporation No. / *(For Corporate Partners Only)*
N° matricule de la personne morale en Ontario *Pour les personnes morales associées seulement*

7. Last Name / Nom de famille   First Name / Prénom   Middle Initial / initiale 2e prénom
GREEN   JACK   G.

8. Street No./ N° de rue   Street Name / Nom de la rue   Suite No. / Bureau n°   City / Town / Ville
28 CAN ZONE DRIVE   SCARBOROUGH

Province / Province   Country / Pays   Postal Code / Code postal
ONTARIO   CANADA   Z1P 0G0

Additional Information. Only complete if the registrant is not an individual. See instructions 7/8 on the form. /
Renseignements supplémentaires. À remplir uniquement si la personne enregistrée n'est pas un particulier.
Voir les instructions 7 et 8 sur le formulaire.

Ont. Corporation No. / *(For Corporate Partners Only)*
N° matricule de la personne morale en Ontario *Pour les personnes morales associées seulement*

9. Print name of person authorizing this registration / *(either the sole proprietor, a partner or a person acting under a power of attorney)*
If the person is a corporation, complete additional information below only. /
Indiquez en lettres majuscules le nom de la personne autorisant l'enregistrement / *(propriétaire unique, associé, ou personne habilitée en vertu d'une procuration). (Si c'est une personne morale qui autorise l'enregistrement, compléter les renseignements supplémentaires ci-dessous).*

Last Name / Nom de famille   First Name / Prénom   Middle Initial / initiale 2e prénom
DOE   JOHN   D.

If person authorizing the registration is not an individual (eg. corporation, trust, syndicate), print name below and do not complete last, first and middle names above. /
Si la personne qui autorise l'enregistrement n'est pas un individu (c'est-à-dire une personne morale, un trust ou syndicat) ne pas remplir le nom de famille, prénom et 2e prénom.

Additional Information / Renseignements supplémentaires

MINISTRY USE ONLY - RÉSERVÉ AU MINISTÈRE

07219 (03/2003)

(a) Is there a sharing of net profits and losses?

(b) Do any of the parties act as agents for the others?

(c) Is there any property held in joint tenancy?

(d) Is there any implication of partnership on your firm's letterhead or in its correspondence?

(e) Is the nature of the work relationship that of a partnership?

2. The corporate entity and advantages to incorporating

Many people prefer to carry on business as a corporation because of its unique characteristics. A corporation is a distinct legal entity, an artificial person quite different from the people who are its shareholders. When you incorporate, you actually create a new person in the eyes of the law. The assets and debts of a corporation belong to it — not to the individual shareholders. Because of this characteristic, there are four major advantages for people who incorporate their business.

(a) There is potentially a greater source of capital available than in a partnership. Since the corporation is a "person" separate from its shareholders, people may invest money in it without accepting any further responsibility for conducting the company business and without worrying about becoming liable for the debts of the "corporation."

(b) Since the corporation is a separate "person," it does not expire when the shareholders die. Substantial estate planning benefits result from this aspect of incorporation.

(c) The most advantageous and unique characteristic of a corporation is its limited liability, and this is why corporations are referred to as "limited companies." The words "Limited,"

"Limitée," "Ltd.," or "Ltée"; "Incorporated," "Incorporée," or "Inc."; "Corporation" or "Corp." must appear in the names of all corporations.

This means that you as a shareholder, with certain exceptions, are not liable for any act, default, obligation, or liability of the corporation. This is obviously an important advantage to you. There are, however, certain practical considerations, the most important one being that, in many instances, creditors, particularly banks, will not extend credit to a small corporation without your personal guarantee as a shareholder. However, if you do not personally guarantee your corporation's loans, then your liability as a shareholder is limited.

The following examples illustrate the foregoing principles:

Example 1

John Doe and Jack Doe carry on business as a partnership known as J & J Industries.

J & J Industries incurs debts of $25 200.00.

The assets of J & J Industries are $10 200.00.

A creditor successfully petitions J & J Industries into bankruptcy or simply gets a judgment against J & J Industries.

All the assets of John Doe and Jack Doe, as individuals, including possibly their homes, cars, etc., may be executed against to repay the $15 200.00 debt incurred by the partnership over and above its assets.

Example 2

John Doe and Jack Doe carry on business as a corporation known as J & J Industries Limited, with John Doe and Jack Doe the only shareholders, each having purchased one share at $1 (although any number of shares can be purchased).

J & J Industries Limited incurs debts of $250 000.

The assets of J & J Industries Limited are considered to have a market value of $100 000.

A creditor successfully petitions J & J Industries Limited into bankruptcy.

The creditors can realize $100 000 on the assets of the corporation but they have no rights against John and Jack as individuals, regardless of the value of personal assets that John and Jack may own outside the corporation. The creditors are creditors of the corporation, not of John and Jack.

In arranging credit with a financial institution, it may be advisable, if not necessary, to arrange for life insurance on the lives of the shareholders. Depending on how the policy is arranged, different income tax consequences may arise, and professional advice should be sought.

(d) The tax advantages of incorporating are so important that a whole chapter has been devoted to the subject (see chapter 2).

To summarize, then, there are three main legal forms an organization can take. These forms and their individual characteristics are outlined briefly below for quick reference.

Proprietorship

(a) Unincorporated

(b) Owned by one person

(c) Creditors have a legal claim on both the investment in the business and the personal assets of the owner

Partnership

(a) Unincorporated

(b) Each partner has unlimited liability in a general partnership arrangement

(c) The acts of one partner in the course of the management of the business are binding on the other partners

(d) The partnership dissolves upon the death or withdrawal of any partner, or upon the acceptance of a new partner

(e) Creditors have a legal claim on both the investment in the business and the personal assets of the owners

Corporation

(a) Incorporated in most provinces by Memorandum of Association or Articles of Incorporation or federally by Articles of Incorporation

(b) Exists as a separate legal entity

(c) Shareholders are not liable for any act, default, obligation, or liability of the corporation, with certain exceptions

(d) May possess tax advantages

3. Disadvantages to incorporating

First, operating through a corporation does entail extra paperwork. You have to maintain minutes of your meetings and written resolutions and keep registers. You have to file two tax returns: one for your corporation and one for yourself. There may be additional government paperwork to do from time to time, which could be avoided by operating as a sole proprietor. Also, there is the cost of setting up and maintaining a minute book and records office (see chapter 5).

Second, any active business income in excess of $200 000 per year does not enjoy the small business tax incentive; income at this level attracts normal corporate tax rates. However, I assume that this situation applies to so few people that further comment is unnecessary.

Third, there is the cost and bother of doing the incorporating. By the time you are finished, you will have spent approximately $500 (in disbursement costs) and a few hours of your time. Is it worth it? Only you can judge.

b. FINANCIAL STATEMENTS AND THEIR IMPORTANCE

Regardless of what the law says and no matter what legal form an organization may take, the preparation of meaningful financial statements is vital to any enterprise. This is because various people will have an interest in the financial affairs of the organization, namely, owners, managers, creditors, Canada Customs and Revenue Agency (CCRA), and prospective buyers.

To illustrate, assume that you are a bank manager and that J & J Industries Limited, a medium-sized corporation in the business of manufacturing, approaches you for a $100 000 loan. The principal explains that the funds are necessary for plant expansion. As a prospective creditor you would be interested in two things: the ability of J & J Industries Limited to pay the regular instalments of principal and interest on the loan and the amount you — the bank — would recover if the corporation could not meet its obligation. To satisfy your curiosity, you would have to examine the financial statements of the corporation. The annual income would be shown on the profit and loss statement. This figure, if compared with the income from prior periods, would indicate to you the rate of economic growth of the enterprise.

In addition you would be able to determine whether or not enough total revenue is generated to repay the proposed loan.

The balance sheet of the corporation would indicate any other long-term debt for which the corporation is liable. Furthermore, you would be able to determine which assets (inventories, accounts receivable, etc.) are available as security for the proposed loan.

The corporation's ability to pay its current obligations is another important indicator of the economic health of the enterprise. This ability to pay present debts when due can also be determined from the balance sheet. This indicator is expressed as a ratio (called the "current ratio") and is calculated by dividing the total of the current assets by the total current liabilities. This is illustrated with the very simple example in Sample 2.

Current assets exceed current liabilities in the ratio of 2:1. In other words, the working capital position of the corporation in this case is healthy.

In summary, you would obtain much of the information so vital to your decision regarding the loan by looking at the financial statements of J & J Industries Limited.

This illustration shows how financial statements can be useful to potential creditors. Furthermore, financial statements are

SAMPLE 2
BALANCE SHEET

J & J INDUSTRIES LIMITED
March 31, 200–

Current Assets		Current Liabilities	
Cash	$ 20 000	Trade payables	$100 000
Accounts receivable	290 000	Wages payable	10 000
Inventories	90 000	Current portion of long term debt	90 000
TOTAL	$400 000	**TOTAL**	$200 000

useful to anyone who has an interest (monetary or otherwise) in an enterprise. As an analogy: just as certain medical implements are the tools by which a doctor can get some indication of physical health, so financial statements are the tools by which interested parties can measure the economic health of an organization.

Below is a breakdown of the three major financial statements: the balance sheet, the profit and loss statement, and the statement of retained earnings. They are discussed here to enable you to get some idea of the function and contents of financial statements.

1. Balance sheet

The balance sheet is a position statement, not a historical record, and shows what the business owns and owes at a given date. There are three sections to a balance sheet: assets, liabilities, and owner's equity.

(a) Assets

Current assets are those that will be used up within one year of the current balance sheet date. Normal valuation of such assets is at original cost or market value, whichever is lower.

Fixed assets are those that will provide benefits to the organization over a longer period than one year from the current balance sheet date. Valuation is generally at original cost less accumulated depreciation. The amount of depreciation is based on the length of the useful life of the asset and the original cost of the asset.

To illustrate:

Building: original cost $20 000

Useful life: 10 years

Portion of asset cost that expires in each period:

$$\frac{\$20\ 000}{10} = \$2\ 000$$

This type of depreciation is normally calculated on a reducing balance basis but for illustrative purposes, I have used the straight line method. The sum of $2 000 is charged to the profit and loss statement in each period and is accumulated on the balance sheet as a reduction of the original cost of the asset. Thus, five years after the building was purchased, the balance sheet would show:

Building, at cost	$20 000
Less accumulated depreciation (5 x $2 000)	10 000
Book value of building	$10 000

Because the asset may be sold for more than the original cost, the book value does not necessarily indicate the amount the equity-holders should receive for their ownership of the building. (**Note:** "Equity-holders" in a corporation are shareholders.)

(b) Liabilities and owner's equity

Liabilities are those things that are owed by the company to others, both on a short-term and a long-term basis, and include things such as accounts payable, bank loans, and unpaid taxes.

Owner's equity is determined by subtracting liabilities from total assets and it represents the value of the owner's shareholding for accounting purposes. This value may very well be different from the fair market value of the owner's shareholding because fair market value can only be determined from what an arm's length purchaser would be prepared to pay for the shareholdings, and not necessarily what the shareholdings are valued at for accounting purposes.

2. Profit and loss statement

This statement indicates the profit or loss by subtracting the total expenses of a period from the total revenue for that period. There are two ways of determining when revenue is earned and when expenses are incurred. They are —

(a) Cash basis — No revenue is recognized until cash is received. No expenses are recognized until cash is paid out.

(b) Accrual basis — Revenue is recognized as soon as it is earned. Expenses are recognized as soon as they are incurred. The date cash is received or paid out is irrelevant.

3. Statement of retained earnings

The statement of retained earnings shows accumulated retained earnings from year to year. Added to the opening balance of retained earnings for the year is the current year's net profit (after income tax). From that sum, dividends declared and paid are subtracted to arrive at a closing balance for the current year.

The closing balance is summarized on the balance sheet in Sample 3 as the entry Retained Earnings and Partners' Equity.

The closing balance for the current year becomes the opening balance for the following year.

c. WHERE TO INCORPORATE

Since a corporation is an artificial person, it must be created by someone. A corporation may be incorporated or "born" by a certificate of incorporation granted under either the Canada Business Corporations Act or the Business Corporations Act (Ontario).

The advantage of incorporating federally is that the corporation has the capacity of a natural person and protection of its corporate name on a nationwide basis. A provincially incorporated corporation has the capacity of a natural person only in the province of incorporation (although there are provisions for registration in other provinces).

For most "non-public" (i.e., small, private, family-owned and operated corporations), it is much more convenient to incorporate a provincial corporation. This book deals with Ontario corporations only.

d. PUBLIC VERSUS PRIVATE CORPORATIONS

For purposes of Ontario corporation law, corporations can be of three types: listed corporations, non-listed offering corporations, or closely held (private) non-offering corporations.

1. Listed corporations

Under this category are included most of the well-known, large public corporations that have stock that is actively traded on one or more recognized stock exchanges. This book does not discuss this type of organization.

2. Non-listed offering corporations

Under this category are included all corporations with shares that are "publicly" held but, for one reason or another, are not listed and traded on a recognized stock exchange. The most common example is the over-the-counter stock.

This book does not cover this type of organization because, technically, such corporations are "public" as far as the Ontario Securities Commission is concerned and, as such, are required to comply with the rules and regulations of the Ontario Securities Commission regarding issuing of prospectuses and other items.

3. Closely held (private) corporations

Obviously, not all corporations are incorporated for the purpose of selling shares and raising large amounts of capital. The general advantages of incorporation are explained earlier in this chapter. A different type of corporation was created by both

SAMPLE 3
BALANCE SHEET FOR UNINCORPORATED BUSINESS

ASSETS

Current Assets

Cash on hand and in bank		$720.12	
Accounts receivable less allowance for doubtful accounts		657.72	
Merchandise inventory valued at the lower of original cost or market		3 212.63	
Prepaid expenses		157.55	
Total current assets			$ 4 748.02

Fixed Asset — At Cost

Land		$2 320.00	
Building	$5 767.16		
Less: accumulated depreciation	1 727.92	4 039.24	
Store fixtures	3 726.12		
Less: accumulated depreciation	982.36	2 743.76	
Delivery truck	2 760.20		
Less: accumulated depreciation	513.60	2 246.60	11 349.60
			$16 097.62

LIABILITIES & PARTNERS' EQUITY

Current Liabilities

Trade Accounts payable	$2 772.18	
Accrued wage	75.20	
Employees' income tax payable	60.16	
Accrued real estate taxes	220.00	
Total current liabilities		$3 127.54

Retained Earnings and Partners' Equity*

Jones's share	$6 484.84	
Smith's share	6 484.84	
		12 969.68
		$16 097.22

*If the company was incorporated, this would read as follows:

CAPITAL STOCKS
Common stock, no par value, maximum selling price $1
Authorized — 10 000 shares

Issued and fully paid for:
Jones — 50 shares at $0.01 = $0.50
Smith — 50 shares at $0.01 = $0.50

Retained earnings $12 969.68

You will note that Jones and Smith still have equity of a total of $12 969.68.

provincial and federal legislation to give small businesses the advantages of incorporation.

Private corporations can be thought of as "incorporated partnerships" rather than as corporations as we normally view them because they usually consist of one, two, or three people who are close personal friends, business associates, or family members.

Another important distinction to keep in mind is that in public corporations the directors, officers, and shareholders are often separate individuals. However, in private corporations, each individual may hold two or three positions in the corporation. For example, it is not unusual for one person to be, at the same time, a shareholder, officer, and director.

The directors on the board of a public corporation are usually a group of businesspeople respected in the community who bring to the board a wide variety of business experience. Their function is to act as "watchdog" over the officers and to protect the shareholders' interest.

Most officers of large public corporations are "hired professionals" and they are in charge of the day-to-day activities. In many instances they also wield the greatest influence on the overall operations of the corporation.

Usually the two or three top officers of the corporation are also members of the board of directors.

The last group in a public corporation, but certainly the largest in terms of numbers, consists of the shareholders. In public corporations, this group is the "owner" of the corporation which, in turn, owns the assets. Shares represent ownership. However, ownership of shares does not usually vest in the shareholder the right or power to run the corporation.

In theory, the final authority for a corporation's operation rests with the shareholders. In the reality of public corporations, shareholders may choose not to exercise this right for many reasons.

Shareholders are often spread all over the country, so very few attend the annual meeting. Most shareholders want only a return on their investment (dividends) and an increase in value of their shares; they do not want to run a corporation. If the corporation does not perform satisfactorily, the shareholders may simply sell their shares rather than call the management or directors to task or replace them. Furthermore, many shareholders lack the competence and business experience necessary to run the business properly so they hesitate to question the activities of managing officers or directors.

Finally, the usual wide dispersal of shareholders means that it would take a great deal of time, money, and effort for a group of reform-minded individuals to obtain enough support to seriously challenge the management or directors of the corporation.

If you were to visualize the hierarchy of a public corporation, it would look like this:

XYZ LTD.

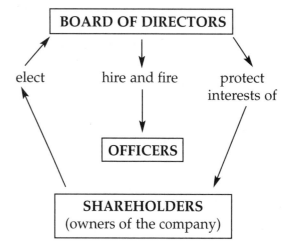

All corporations must have directors, officers, and shareholders. One distinction between public and private corporations is that in public corporations these positions are generally occupied by different persons. A vice-president in a public corporation may not necessarily be on the board of directors and will generally not own enough shares of the corporation to affect corporate policy from a shareholder's position. His or her effect on the operations of the corporation will derive solely from his or her position as an officer of the corporation.

In a private corporation, these positions are usually occupied by the same people. For example, if you have a "family" corporation in which the husband has 50 percent of the shares, the wife 25 percent, and a son the other 25 percent, it is likely that these people will be the sole directors.

You need at least one director as well as two officers. Be careful not to confuse these positions, even though the people occupying them are the same. In a private corporation, you are often wearing more than one hat at the same time.

To illustrate, in the day-to-day activities of your small business, you are wearing the hat of an officer. If you decide, however, to branch out into a new area or to purchase or sell significant assets, you are wearing the hat of a director. (Important matters that will have considerable effect on the corporation are usually referred to the board of directors.) When you attend and vote at the annual meeting, or buy or sell shares, you are acting as a shareholder. The shareholder always has the final say on any serious issue because shareholdings represent ownership of the corporation.

You will find instances in which "partners" in a business on a day-to-day level are not 50/50 owners of a corporation on a shareholding basis. This is one of the great dangers of incorporating a small business. The minority shareholder (less than 50 percent) is usually in a precarious position in relation to the majority shareholder (more than 50 percent).

I suggest that if you are in an incorporated "partnership" with another person who is not related to you that you prepare and execute a shareholders' agreement that lays out the rules for the everyday management of the corporation.

You might ask what will happen when there is a basic disagreement over some issue and a deadlock results. The answer is that either the assets are sold and the business is wound up or one party buys out the other. This reflects the basic nature of a private corporation, which is that of an incorporated "partnership."

We all know what happens when partners in a business have an irreconcilable difference. The same is true in a small corporation. But a 50/50 split of the shares does encourage co-operation. When this balance is altered it will, of necessity, affect the personal relationship of the "partners."

Remember, this book discusses only those corporations not offering securities to the public. The distinction between corporations that offer securities to the public and corporations that do not is important and must be continually borne in mind, particularly in the case of growing organizations seeking alternative methods of raising capital financing.

e. ONE-PERSON CORPORATIONS

Both the Canada Business Corporations Act and the Business Corporations Act (Ontario) allow the formation of a one-person corporation. This means that one person may be the president and secretary, sole director, and sole shareholder.

The evolution of one-person corporations recognizes that many persons are in business solely for themselves. (This is the so-called incorporated proprietorship.)

The procedures for incorporation are essentially the same for the one-person corporation as for the two-or-more-person corporation, but from a practical standpoint, the one-person corporation generally approves corporate transactions by passing a director's resolution rather than by holding a meeting (see chapter 5 for further details).

f. HOW MANY SHARES SHOULD YOU ISSUE?

After the new corporation is incorporated and organized, it will require financing in order to begin operations. Capital flows into a business in two ways:

(a) By investing in shares (i.e., equity capital)

(b) By lending money to the business in some form or other (i.e., shareholder loans, bonds, debentures)

There are some definite advantages to capitalizing a business through loans, as opposed to buying shares, especially a high-risk business such as a newly "incorporated partnership."

First, capital "loaned" to the corporation, as opposed to "invested" in the corporation, can be repaid at any time tax free. That is, a loan to the corporation repaid to a shareholder is not income to the shareholder.

On the other hand, money invested in shares usually can't be repaid without tax consequences.

Second, if the new corporation is in financial difficulty, a shareholder loan will generally rank equally with the other creditors when dividing up the remainder of the assets and ranks ahead of repayment to the shareholders for money invested in shares. Common shareholders rarely see any proceeds when a corporation goes bankrupt or goes out of business.

Third, by minimizing the number of shares, you keep the initial capital investment at a minimum.

There is simply no advantage in financing the corporation by issuing shares only. There is no real need in most simple incorporation situations to issue immediately all of the shares that you incorporated with to shareholders. The unissued shares remain in the company treasury and belong to the corporation itself until it becomes necessary to issue them to new shareholders. Just visualize all unissued shares as sitting in a large pot labelled "Company treasury" until directors' minutes issuing them to new shareholders are drawn up and filed in the minute book.

If a corporation is incorporated with an unlimited number of shares, and there are only two shareholders, then, for example, only one share needs to be issued to each of them. If they each have an equal number of the issued shares, their interests are the same as if they had each taken 5 000 of the corporation's shares.

If you look ahead in the book at the model set of Articles of Incorporation (see Sample 9 in chapter 3), you will see that the sample corporation is capitalized with an unlimited number of shares. Out of this "pool" 9 shares have been issued to the incorporator, John Doe, for a price of $10, which should be deposited into the corporation's bank account.

As an alternative to issuing only 10 shares, you may want to consider issuing 1 000 shares at 10 cents per share. This way, it will be easier to sell any of these shares to another person because each share will have a lower value than if only 10 shares were issued. Similarly, it will be easier for a newcomer to your corporation to subscribe for shares from the company treasury since each share would have a lower value than if only 10 shares had been issued initially.

A final and most important reason for limiting the number of shares you issue is that, if your business is successful, you may wish to bring in other "partners" who want to invest in the business. At that time a valuation of the amount of "equity" you have in the business will have to be made by your accountant.

Equity is defined as assets minus liabilities and represents the net worth of the business. From the examples here you can see that it makes no difference how many total shares are issued as long as your position in relation to other shareholders is not altered. Also, by keeping most of the shares in the treasury, you will be flexible enough to meet new corporation developments.

Samples 4 and 5 are balance sheets for a corporation where the number of shares issued to shareholders is 10 and 10 000 respectively. I have purposely simplified matters by deducting shareholders' contributions in each case because this is like transferring money from one hand to the next in a small, non-public corporation. I have also deliberately ignored the "good will" or capitalization of earnings factor which merely serves to place a multiple factor on the net earnings.

As you can see in Samples 4 and 5, John Doe's business is worth the same on a net return basis.

Another common situation is where another shareholder is brought in. In such a case you have two alternatives to consider.

First, you may simply transfer a percentage of each of the existing shareholder's holdings to the new "partner." If the shares are sold for more than you paid for them you will have to think about the capital gains tax liability.

Another problem with this method is that frequently you end up with a fractional share situation which is always annoying to deal with, to say the least.

For example, suppose John and Jack Doe each own 50 shares. Their cousin, Helen, becomes involved and all parties agree that she should be an equal shareholder. To do this, both Jack and John would have to transfer $16^2/_3$ shares to Helen and each party would be left with $33^1/_3$ shares, which is an awkward situation.

A better solution would be to issue 25 more shares each to John and Jack Doe and then transfer them to Helen. Again, capital gains tax would have to be considered if the shares are transferred at a higher price than they were issued for.

If, on the other hand, the shares were issued at, say, $5 per share and this amount was paid into the corporation and the shares were then transferred for the same amount, then no tax would be payable.

The other alternative is to issue additional shares directly from the treasury to Helen at the price agreed upon. In this case, no capital gains tax would be payable because the money simply flows into the capital account of the corporation.

Of course, there would also be no direct benefit to John and Jack in bringing Helen in, other than her contribution to the work effort. In other words, the corporation would have additional funds with which to finance its activities, but Jack and John could not receive any financial benefit from Helen's purchase without paying tax.

In most cases, then, it is simpler to issue additional shares, either directly to the new shareholder, or to the existing members first and then transfer them to the new partner, rather than get involved in complicated partial share arrangements.

To recap briefly, since there is no particular advantage to issuing all the shares unless you are involved in a complicated share control problem, and there are several disadvantages to capitalizing through share capital, it is wise to issue a minimum to begin with — for example, 100 to 1 000 shares to each shareholder depending on the number of persons involved.

I have already covered the advantages of financing the corporation through loans rather than equity. You lend the corporation capital by simply writing a cheque and making a note on the cheque and bank deposit slip that it is a shareholder's loan. You can further record the fact that it is a shareholder's loan by drawing up directors' minutes and a demand promissory note for its repayment. (See chapter 5 on post-incorporation procedures.) Your accountant or bookkeeper can make the proper entries from your cheque stubs.

g. CLASSES OF SHARES

As most small private corporations have no need for different classes of shares, you may ignore this section unless you are curious. Generally speaking, shares can have various rights and restrictions attached to them. A *class* of shares can be any set of shares that has attached to it rights different from the rights attached to another set of shares.

For example, when you start your business, you should incorporate with and issue "common shares" to all of the incorporators, so that all the shareholders of the corporation have equal rights to vote and receive dividends. When your corporation becomes successful, you might wish to create a different class of shares which, when issued to shareholders, will give them the right to receive dividends before holders of any other class of shares, or which have cumulative dividend rights, or rights to be redeemed by the corporation. You might refer to the new class of shares as "preferred" shares in order to distinguish them from the other shares that you first issued from the treasury pool. Large public corporations usually have different classes of shares.

Remember, it is much easier to add rights and restrictions at a later date rather than attach them now and then have to buy them up or strip them. If you later wish to create classes of shares that have different rights attached to them, you should see a lawyer so you can carry out the alterations of your Articles correctly and design your capital structure properly to minimize taxes and maximize control.

SAMPLE 4
BALANCE SHEET
(Where 10 shares are issued)

JOE DOE & ASSOCIATES LTD.

ASSETS		LIABILITIES	
Cash	$ 10	Note to the bank	$2 000
Inventory	4 000	Shareholder loan	3 000
Building	5 000		
Total assets	$9 010	Total liability	$5 000

NET WORTH

Capital stock authorized — unlimited shares	
Issued 10 shares at $1.00 each	$ 10
Retail earnings	4 000
Total liability and equity	$9 010

Note: The corporation has earned $4 000 to date. Each share is worth $401 (total net worth divided by 10) but as $1 of this amount is shareholders' money and it is really a matter of transferring it from one hand to the other, it really should not be included in determining the value of the corporation from the shareholder's point of view. Therefore, if the assets of the corporation were liquidated tomorrow it would be worth $4 000 in *net return* to the shareholders.

SAMPLE 5
BALANCE SHEET
(Where 10 000 shares are issued)

JOE DOE & ASSOCIATES LTD.

ASSETS		LIABILITIES	
Cash	$40 000	Note to the bank	$2 000
Inventory	4 000	Shareholder loan	3 000
Building	5 000		
Total assets	$49 000	Total liability	$5 000

NET WORTH

Capital stock authorized — unlimited shares	
Issued 10 000 shares at $4.00 each to John Doe	$40 000
Retail earnings	4 000
Total liability and equity	$49 000

Note: If the business is wound up, John Doe's shares are worth 44 000 but $40 000 of this is John Doe's own money. Therefore, the net return would again be $4 000.

2
TAX ADVANTAGES TO INCORPORATING

There can be substantial tax advantages to incorporating your business. This chapter outlines the major ones.

a. BASIC CORPORATE RATE*

The basic combined federal and Ontario corporate income tax rate before the small business deduction and manufacturing and processing credit is approximately 36.6 percent. The rate on income from manufacturing operations is about 33.1 percent. Federal and Ontario corporate tax rates have dropped substantially over the past few years and are scheduled to be further reduced over the next few years.

b. QUALIFYING FOR THE SMALL BUSINESS TAX RATE*

Provided your business can qualify for the small business rate, your corporation can receive a substantial reduction in taxes payable on active business earnings. The combined federal and provincial tax rate for the first $200 000 of net income from an active business carried on in Canada is about 18.6 percent. The 2003 federal budget proposes to increase the $200 000 small business limit by $25 000 a year commencing in 2003 until it reaches $300 000 in 2006. The Ontario small business limit is presently $320 000 and will increase to $360 000 in 2004 and to $400 000 in 2005. However, the benefit is reduced as net income moves above the small-business limit. The "claw back" of the tax benefit is different for different tax regimes, but at $800 000 of taxable income per annum, the benefit of the small-business tax rate will be totally eliminated for Ontario provincial tax purposes.

As discussed above, as a result of various Ontario budgets, the $200 000 limit is being increased gradually until it reaches $400 000 in 2005. The clawback is being correspondingly increased so that in 2005 the benefit of the small-business deduction will be totally limited for Ontario tax purposes when income reaches $1 000 000. One method of keeping the corporation's income within the small-business limit is to pay bonuses annually to yourself of the income in excess of the small-business limit. This bonus is deductible to the corporation and will be included in your income as discussed below.

To qualify for the small-business rate on net income up to the small business limit from an active business, there are certain tests to meet:

(a) Your corporation must be a Canadian-controlled private corporation; that is, a private Canadian corporation other than a corporation controlled either directly or indirectly by one or more non-residents or by one or more public corporations or by any such combination.

(b) Only income from an active business carried on in Canada is eligible for the low rate.

(c) Corporations that are "associated" with the corporation in question must share the benefit of the small-business tax rate.

If the corporation fails any of these tests, then the tax rate will be between approximately 33 percent and 36 percent (subject to further reduction as described above)

*All rates shown assume that you reside in Ontario.

16

depending on whether the income is from manufacturing and processing or not.

Any business carried on by your corporation will be considered active with two exceptions: personal services business (which refers to a business of providing personal services that would ordinarily be provided to the recipient by an individual employee rather than by a corporation) and investment businesses. Personal service corporations are held ineligible in order to prevent an individual who incorporates to obtain the benefit of lower taxes when, in fact, he or she could be considered an "employee" of the corporation paying the remuneration. This type of corporation usually has income from one main source and has five or less employees. If you are contemplating forming a corporation to provide personal services, you should obtain professional advice.

Personal services businesses and investment businesses will be taxed at the regular rate, not the small business rate, unless the corporation has six or more full-time employees throughout the year or if, in the case of a management services corporation, it receives its income from a corporation associated with it. In such cases, investment corporations and "incorporated employees" will both be eligible for the low tax rate.

Assuming you qualify for the small-business rate, the tax advantages to incorporating are outlined below.

c. SPLIT YOUR INCOME

With a corporation, you can effectively "split" your income. For example, say your business made $125 000 last year as a proprietorship. This entire amount would be considered your personal income and be taxed on an ascending scale up to about 46 percent. (This rate may be greater or less depending on the province in which you reside.)

On the other hand, if you have incorporated, for example, $25 000 could be paid to you personally as salary or bonus and $100 000 could be left in the corporation. This $100 000 would be taxed at the rate of about 18.6 percent if your corporation qualifies for the small business tax rate.

The $25 000 paid to you personally would be subject to tax at the low end of the individual tax rate scale (the marginal tax rate on the next dollar you would earn would be approximately 22 percent). Thus, the entire $125 000 of income would avoid being subject to tax at high marginal rates. Note, however, that RRSP contributions will be limited by the reduced salary amount and this will offset the tax rate savings.

This is just one example. In fact, you are allowed to work out any combination that keeps your total tax bill to a minimum, including employing members of your family. However, the payment received by family members must reasonably reflect the market value of the services provided.

A further split is also possible. After paying this initial corporate tax, you can then choose either to leave the funds in the corporation or to pay out dividends to the shareholders (you, your spouse, and children). Special attribution rules exist that can function to tax dividends received by family members in your hands unless the arrangement is properly structured. As a result of recent amendments, there are now rules that tax dividends received by children under 18 years of age at the top marginal tax rate, thereby rendering such income splitting with minors impractical. Professional advice should be sought in structuring this type of arrangement.

Depending upon the sources and level of your income, subject to the comments in the previous paragraph, it may be more advantageous for one or more of your family members to take payments from the corporation in the form of dividends alone or in a mixture of dividends and salary. An individual resident in Ontario with no other sources of income will be able to receive approximately $28 975 of Canadian dividends without being subject to tax. This is because of the dividend tax credit. The corporation must be carefully structured for this technique to work properly.

However, since dividends are not deductible and it is important to limit, if at all possible, net corporate business income to the small-business limit discussed above in order to pay the lowest corporate income tax rate, payments of bonuses and salary as described below may be preferable to dividends.

As noted above, one critical point to keep in mind is that dividend income does not qualify as "earned income" for purposes of making a deductible contribution to an RRSP. Thus, if your entire income consisted of dividends, you would not get a deduction for any contribution to your RRSP. Furthermore, your income might also be subject to the alternative minimum tax.

d. ESTATE PLANNING BENEFITS

With a corporation, you can effect substantial estate planning advantages. As this is a technical area and beyond the scope of this book, it will not be discussed at any length. Suffice it to say that the existence of a corporation enables you to hold a widely diversified portfolio of assets (including all kinds of property) in a single entity.

This can be a great advantage from both a tax and an administrative point of view, for instance, if the corporation is located in a jurisdiction like Ontario that does not have estate taxes while the assets are located in a jurisdiction that does (e.g., the United States).

e. CAPITAL GAINS EXEMPTION

The sale of business assets held personally will generally trigger an immediate tax liability if the tax cost base of the assets is below the selling price. If the shares of a corporation that carries on the business are sold instead of the assets, the shareholder/vendor may be entitled to the special $500 000 tax-free capital gains exemption for certain qualifying small-business shares. The same tax-free capital gains exemption can be realized if qualifying shares are gifted or willed to family members. Complex rules govern this tax-free capital gains exemption and your tax advisor can assist you in this area.

f. USE SALARY AND BONUS ACCRUALS

Your corporation can declare a bonus payable to you that is deductible in computing the corporation's income but need not be declared by you as income until it is actually paid. However, the Income Tax Act (Canada) provides that the bonus has to be paid within 180 days from the end of your corporation's tax year in which the bonus was declared in order for the corporation to claim the deduction in the year in which the bonus was declared. For example, if your corporation's year end was December 31 and on December 31, 2003, it declared a bonus payable to you of $10 000, the corporation could deduct it as an expense for the 2003 taxation year only if the bonus was actually paid to you by June 28, 2004. The result is that you would pay personal tax on the bonus in your 2004 taxation year. If the bonus was paid after that date, the corporation would deduct the bonus in the year in which it was paid to you.

You can see that this gives you some flexibility. To be deductible, these bonuses must be reasonable (in relation to services rendered to the corporation) and represent a legal liability of the corporation. (Passing a directors' resolution before the corporation's year end is advisable.)

In addition, there are other tax issues such as the Ontario employer health tax and other payroll taxes that will affect decisions relating to the salary/dividend/

bonus mix which a tax adviser can tell you about.

The important thing to remember is that you must be careful in planning bonuses to look at the overall tax liability of both you and your corporation. If your corporation is already able to take advantage of the low small-business tax rate, there is little sense in declaring a bonus that will be taxed in your hands as regular income at a higher rate.

If you want to reduce your corporation's earnings so that it can take advantage of the small-business rate, you might want to declare a bonus payable to yourself so as to reduce the corporation's active business income below the small-business limit discussed above and wait before paying it as described above.

Furthermore, by reducing your corporate profits, you reduce the size of the tax instalment payments payable by the corporation and, therefore, improve its cash flow position.

If you declare dividends payable to yourself, there is no time limit on when they can be paid to you. Once the corporation has paid tax on its profits, dividends can be distributed at any time. This might be beneficial from the point of view of liability for personal income tax.

Remember, whichever method you choose to distribute your corporate earnings, it must be designed to meet the monetary needs and tax liabilities of both you and the corporation.

g. EXPENSE DEDUCTIONS

Aside from the fact that operating your business through a corporation may, as a practical matter, allow you to claim more liberal travel and entertainment expenses, there are perfectly legal and sanctioned ways of using a corporation to increase expense allowances. For example, country club and similar dues paid by your corporation on your behalf, while not tax deductible by the corporation, do not have to be included in your personal income, provided you use the clubs for business entertainment. Therefore, because the corporation is taxed at a lower rate than you personally, it can earn less than you to net the same amount.

Similarly, if you are arranging life insurance policies, the corporation can own the policy and pay the premiums (non-deductible — but the money earned to pay the premium is taxed at a lower rate) and any proceeds collected by the corporation are non-taxable to the corporation and may be distributed to shareholders as a tax-free capital dividend.

h. PLANNING FOR YOUR RETIREMENT

In the past, the opportunity for small business owners to provide for their own retirement was exceptional. Unfortunately, that is no longer the case.

If you are an owner/employee of a corporation, you may not be a beneficiary of your corporation's deferred profit-sharing plan ("DPSP"). If the corporation does not have a DPSP or a registered pension plan ("RPP"), or you are not a beneficiary, your maximum contribution to a registered retirement savings plan can be 18 percent of your earned income up to specified limits. The current limit is $14 500. Check with your local Canada Customs and Revenue Agency office (the phone number is listed in the blue pages of your phone book) for changes.

Retiring allowances given to employees or employee/shareholders can be transferred to an RRSP, but are limited to years of service before 1996. For years of service between 1989 and 1995 inclusive, the transfer is limited to $2 000 per year of service. For years of service commencing before

1989, an additional $1 500 per year of service may be transferred for each year the employee did not have vested rights under an RPP or DPSP. Provided the amount paid is reasonable, the corporation can deduct retirement allowance payments.

i. LOANS TO EMPLOYEES AND SHAREHOLDERS

Loans made by a corporation to employees or shareholders that have a below market rate of interest or are non-interest bearing will create a taxable benefit to the employee or shareholder. The taxable benefit will be equal to the difference between the interest rate charged to the employee and the prescribed rate set by the government.

This rate is adjusted quarterly based on the interest rate paid on 91-day treasury bills for the previous quarter. In other words, on a no-interest loan of $10 000, $300 is added to the employee's income if the prescribed rate is 3 percent.

However, on loans to purchase shares in their employer corporation, employees will be able to deduct the deemed interest expense against all other employment income or income from property and dividends, provided the shares bought are either preferred shares that yield taxable dividends higher than the prescribed interest rate or common shares. Thus, no net benefit will be included in the employee's income. It should be noted, however, that to the extent that an employee's interest expense exceeds income from property (e.g., interest and dividends, etc.), it will effectively reduce any immediate access to the capital gains exemption by the amount of such excess until such excess is ultimately absorbed by income from property.

Where the loan is made to allow the employee to buy a car to be used on the job, there are complex rules regarding the interest costs, depreciation, possible taxable benefits, and GST. Your tax advisor should be consulted on any questions of employer-owned or leased vehicles versus employee-provided vehicles.

Special rules also apply if a loan to a shareholder is not repaid within a certain period of time. Subject to certain exceptions, a loan to a shareholder will be included in the shareholder's income when received unless it is repaid within one year from the end of the taxation year of the corporation in which the loan was made and was not part of a series of loans and repayments.

j. MANUFACTURING AND PROCESSING CREDIT (M&P)

For income not eligible for the small-business rate, the M&P credit will reduce the rate of tax on manufacturing income not eligible for the small-business rate to about 33 percent in Ontario.

The M&P credit was introduced to reward the capital intensive and internationally competitive manufacturing sector. The Income Tax Act (Canada) specifically disqualifies certain activities. They are farming, fishing, logging, on-site job construction, most natural resource activities, and any manufacturing endeavour where manufacturing revenues are less than 10 percent of the gross sales. Businesses that convert, change, add to, or re-assemble the raw material may qualify. For example, newspapers or printing businesses qualify.

If your business is primarily manufacturing and processing in Canada, did not carry on active business outside the country in the year, and did not carry on activities specifically excluded from the definition of manufacturing and processing, your corporation's income may qualify for this credit.

k. ANTI-AVOIDANCE

There now exists a General Anti-Avoidance Rule (GAAR). Any transaction that results in a significant reduction or even deferral of the tax that might have been payable had the transaction not occurred can be completely ignored unless it can be shown to have had a bona fide non-tax purpose. This rule will generally not be applied to prohibit access to certain specified tax incentives, including the small business deduction and the manufacturing and processing tax credit. Therefore, a business person is free to use a corporate vehicle to access these special tax incentives.

l. CONCLUSION

The realization that profits mean taxes tends to cause businesspeople to overreact and become more and more committed to minimizing their tax load. This is totally understandable and perfectly acceptable, as long as the methods used are legal.

The best way of achieving the lowest possible taxes is to maintain proper and accurate records and ensure that you have at your disposal the legal and accounting expertise you require to assist you in taking advantage of all of the opportunities available under the current tax laws.

3
INCORPORATION PROCEDURE FOR AN ONTARIO CORPORATION NOT OFFERING ITS SECURITIES TO THE PUBLIC

a. SUMMARY OF PROCEDURES

Every person incorporating a corporation should purchase the latest edition of the Business Corporations Act (Ontario). While many acts are difficult to understand, the Business Corporations Act (Ontario) is clearly written and well indexed and organized. It may be purchased from the Queen's Printer (provincial government) in Toronto.

For other pertinent information of a preliminary nature contact:

Ministry of Consumer and
   Business Services
393 University Avenue, Suite 200
Toronto, ON M5G 2M2
Telephone: (416) 314-8880 or
   1-800-361-3223 (outside Toronto but
   in Ontario)
E-mail: cbsinfo@cbs.gov.on.ca

Hours: 8:30 a.m. to 5:00 p.m., Monday through Friday.

The fee which must accompany any application for incorporation may be found in the Schedule to the Regulations at the end of the Ontario Business Corporations Act. The section applicable to incorporating fees is reproduced in Table 1.

The following is a general, abbreviated, step-by-step list of the procedures necessary to incorporate a business corporation in Ontario.

Each of these steps is discussed in detail in the sections of the book following.

(a) Select a name and submit it to a name search firm.

(b) Once your name is approved, complete and file —

   (i)   duplicate copies of the Articles of Incorporation,

TABLE 1
SCHEDULE OF FEES

Filing Articles of Incorporation and endorsing a certificate	$360
Filing and issue of certificate to restated Articles of Incorporation	$150
Filing and issue of certificate for Articles of Amendment	$150
Filing Articles of Arrangement and endorsing a certiificate	$330
Filing articles of revival and endorsing a certificate	$330
Filing Articles of Dissolution and endorsing a Certificate	$ 25

Note: All cheques must be certified and made payable to the Minister of Finance.

(ii) any needed consent forms, and

(iii) any name search forms forwarded to you by a name search company.

(c) Send all of the above to the Director, Companies and Personal Property Security Branch (CPPSB), along with a certified cheque for incorporation fees payable to the Minister of Finance.

(d) When your papers have been approved, the Director will issue a Certificate of Incorporation and return to you a certified copy of the Articles. He will also publish the appropriate notice in the Ontario *Gazette.*

(e) Purchase a minute book, share certificates, and corporation seal.

(f) Make banking arrangements with your bank.

(g) Prepare organizational resolutions of directors and shareholders including the banking resolutions.

(h) Insert Certificate of Incorporation, by-laws, and resolutions of shareholders and directors in the minute book.

(i) Issue share certificates.

(j) Complete registers in minute book.

b. CHOOSING A NAME

A corporation, like a person, must have a name, but unfortunately it is not as easy to pick a name for a corporation as it is for a new baby. When you select a name for your corporation, you must consider certain definite factors, the most important one being that the name must be acceptable to the Director, CPPSB. In broad terms, the Director will approve any name that is not identical to any existing corporation names; however, the principals of a corporation assume the risk and responsibility of the name conforming to law.

You are responsible for selecting a name that complies with the Business Corporations Act (Ontario) and that you are entitled to use. You do not want to be required at some later date to change your name.

With this in mind you should try for one that is distinctive and accurately describes the type of business that you intend to carry on. For example, a name like "Quiggly Cleaners Ltd." would be a better name for a drycleaning company than "Eastern Enterprises Ltd." The word "Eastern" is one of those words that has been so frequently used in names that it is no longer distinctive. Some other words that have met the same fate are "Northern," "Pacific," "Universal," and "Maple Leaf." The word "enterprises" does not describe the business of this particular corporation, although it might be used accurately in naming an investment corporation of some sort.

One of the easiest ways to check existing names is to look in the White Pages and the Yellow Pages for the names of corporations already doing business in your area. Trade and corporation directories which are available in any large library will help you find other protected names of Canadian organizations.

Generally, you should remember that successful proposals are likely to be —

(a) a coined word (perhaps a combination of incorporators' names) plus a descriptive word,

(b) the full name of an individual (e.g., John Albert Doe Ltd.),

(c) the name of an individual combined with a descriptive word, (e.g., Doe Explorations Ltd.), or

(d) the combination of a distinctive geographic name plus a descriptive word (e.g., Niagara Machine Works Ltd.) provided the corporation is connected with or operating in that area.

Of course, all proposals must end with the words "Limited," "Limitée," "Incorporated," "Incorporée," "Corporation," or the abbreviation of these words.

You can set out your corporate name in an English form, a French form, an English form and a French form, or a combined English and French form, and it may be legally designated by any such name.

Only letters from the English alphabet or Arabic numerals or combination thereof, together with the necessary punctuation marks, may form part of the corporate name.

In selecting your name, you should avoid using words like "Condominium" or "Co-operative," which are restricted to specific organizations in many provinces.

Furthermore, you should not use any names that imply a connection with or approval by the royal family. Names using words like "Imperial" or "Royal" will be rejected. Finally, names that imply government approval or the sponsorship of a branch, service, or department are frequently not acceptable. That eliminates words like "Parliament Hill," "RCMP," and "legislative" from the list of choices.

In addition, you should know that you may not receive approval for a name that could possibly be construed as obscene or that is too general in that it only describes the quality, goods, or function of the services. Corporations with names like "General Motors" and "Best Foods" have more or less taken up these choices.

Stay away from the names of corporations already in existence (or the common contractions of their names). For example, a name like Xerox Construction Ltd. implies that your resources are connected with those of Xerox. This is okay if you can show that it is true. If it is not, you may be found liable of trying to "steal" the name in a "passing off" action brought by Xerox. You may also run into difficulties if you choose a name like Inco Investments Ltd.

The word "Inco" is a commonly used contraction for the International Nickel Company of Canada Ltd.

For additional information on restricted words or expressions regarding a corporation's name, see the Business Corporations Act (Ontario) Reg. #62.

While you might think it is easier and more prestigious to give your corporation your own name, there are a few pitfalls that you should be aware of. If you decide to sell your corporation, your name, with its good will and business reputation, goes with it to the new owner, unless, of course, you want to take a considerable loss on the sale price. Suppose the new owner doesn't have your head for business and the corporation with your name on it goes bankrupt. You may have some embarrassing moments when people first meet you and inquire whether or not you are the John Doe who went bankrupt a few years ago while owing his brother-in-law $10 000. It is a small world and people have long memories for this sort of thing.

A further disadvantage to using your own name for a corporation dealing with the public is that people cannot immediately tell what type of business you are in so potential customers may be deterred. Corporations that intend to rely on the general public for business (as opposed to family holding corporations) should have a name that informs the public of the goods or services they offer.

Customer resistance to the idea of doing business with a "large, impersonal corporation" can be overcome by good service and an appealing corporate name. You may wish to seek professional advice from name search companies that assist in selecting a corporation name.

As a general rule, the name of an individual, such as John Doe Inc., will be granted provided it is not similar to an existing corporate name and John Doe's consent accompanies the application.

For example, in this case, if you are John Doe, you simply complete the form shown as Sample 11, the Consent by Individual.

c. CHECKING YOUR NAME

Before you submit your incorporating documents, you should first have your name checked by an Ontario name search firm. The Companies and Personal Property Security Branch (CPPSB) does not search and reserve proposed names. It is your responsibility to obtain a name search report from a private search company, decide on the availability of your proposed name, and ensure that your Articles meet the requirements of the act.

If the name is unimportant to you, or if you really are in a hurry to incorporate, you can submit your documents with a blank space for the name followed by the words, "Ontario Limited" and the CPPSB will assign a number name to your corporation.

In most instances you will want a name that is pleasing to the public, so you would be wise to check out names and choose the one that is available. Take care in making your choice; amending your corporation's name later requires a special procedure set out in the act and additional fees.

The proposed name, or preferably three proposed names, in order of your preference should be submitted to a name search firm in a letter. An example of such a letter appears in Sample 6.

The name search firms use their own computer terminals to scan the information contained in computers operated by the federal and Ontario governments concerning business and corporate names. They charge a fee of approximately $25 for each name search. They will send you a form and a five-page computer printout listing existing corporations with similar names (see Samples 7 and 8). The computer printout listing must be sent to the CPPSB with your Articles.

While the computer printout will assist you in determining that your corporate name is not the same as or similar to another corporation, it does not guarantee that your name is protected from any future proceedings. After you have incorporated, if it is determined that the name you selected is similar to another name, you may be required to change yours.

Furthermore, the protection afforded to your name upon incorporation extends only throughout Ontario. If you are considering doing business across Canada, you should seek professional advice on the merits of trademark protection, or incorporation as a federal company.

Finally, you must file your Articles of Incorporation along with your printout within 90 days of doing your name search and receiving the printout.

The name search firm must use the NUANS system for computer reports.

For a free brochure or further information concerning the services offered by these corporations you may contact them at the addresses listed here.

TORONTO

Best Ontario Inc.
425 University Avenue Suite 403
Toronto, ON M5G 1T6
Telephone: (416) 977-8595
Web site: www.bestontario.com

Dye & Durham Co. Ltd.
439 University Avenue, Suite 1600
Toronto, ON M5G 1Y8
Telephone: (416) 595-7177
Web site: www.dyedurham.ca

Legal Link Inc.
110 Spadina Avenue, Suite 201
Toronto, ON M5V 2K4
Telephone: (416) 348-0432
Web site: www.legallink.ca

Idealogic Searchouse
20 Eglinton Avenue West, Suite 1300
Toronto, ON M4R 1K8
Telephone: (416) 506-9900
Web site: www.idealogic.com

Business Ties Inc. (NCNC)
1033 Bay Street Suite 312
Toronto, ON M5S 3A5
Telephone: (416) 923-4080 or
1-800-268-7580 (in Ontario)

LONDON

Legal Link Inc.
355 Ridout Street North
London, ON N6A 2N8
Telephone: (519) 673-3295
Web site: www.legallink.ca

OTTAWA

House of Selective Researchers Inc./
Maison de Recherches S,lectives Inc.
504 Kent Street
Ottawa, ON K2P 2B9
Telephone: (613) 236-3841

d.   BUSINESS NAMES

Many businesses have a business or "trade" name that is different from the name of their corporation. The main reason for this is that the business name is more easily remembered and is more effective for advertising purposes.

If you have registered and you use a name other than your corporate name, you are required to use the corporate name and your registered name on all contracts, invoices, negotiable instruments, and orders for goods or services.

The Business Names Act (Ontario) deals with, among other things, corporations which carry on business in Ontario under names other than their corporate names. In particular, these corporations are required to register the names under which they carry on business with the CPPSB, and the registration endures for five years, subject to renewal.

A corporation failing to register the name under which it carries on business is unable to maintain an action or proceeding in an Ontario court except with the permission of the court. The court will grant such permission if the failure to register was inadvertent, if there is no indication of deception, or if the corporation then registers the name.

A corporation that violates the Business Names Act (Ontario) by failing to register a name under which it carries on business may be subject to a fine not exceeding $25 000, and its directors and officers to a fine not exceeding $2 000.

You can pick up or order the Statement of Name Registration at 393 University Avenue, Toronto. It will cost you $80 to register it and should be done at the same time as you are incorporating. Sample 8 is an example of the statement. This form, together with your Articles of Incorporation and other materials, may be sent in to the CPPSB, or may be electronically obtained through an authorized provider for an additional fee. It can also be registered after your corporation has been incorporated.

The fee for registering a business name via Ontario Business Connects (OBC) self-help workstations (service time is immediate) or Web site (service time is two weeks) is $60. To obtain the nearest self-help office which gives information and advice on starting and managing your business, or for information on federal and provincial government services and programs, please call the Canada-Ontario Business Service Centre Help Line at (416) 954-4636.

e. BUSINESS LICENCE

A business licence is required by particular businesses in order to operate in Ontario. This is in addition to the Business Name Registration. For example, "Joe's Garage" is required to register its business name with the CPPSB and obtain a licence in order to operate as a garage. To determine if your business will be affected by local regulations, licences, municipal business tax, or zoning requirements contact the clerk of the city, town, village, or rural municipality in which your business will be located. When registering your business name through any of the OBC workstations or at CPPSB, you will receive a Master Business Licence (MBL) following registration. The MBL can be used as proof of business name registration at financial institutions and to facilitate any other business related registration with the Ontario government. The one licence will eventually replace many of the government forms, licences, and certificates held by businesses.

f. DRAFTING THE ARTICLES OF INCORPORATION

Application for the incorporation of a business in Ontario, excluding special types of corporations such as insurance companies, loan and trust companies, corporations without share capital (charitable and non-profit organizations), credit unions, co-operatives, and finance and acceptance companies, is made by submitting duplicate, signed, and dated copies of Articles of Incorporation to the CPPSB. As with business names above, a corporation may also be incorporated electronically.

If the Articles conform to law and are accompanied by the necessary approvals, they will be filed by the Director under the act, who will issue a Certificate of Incorporation. The certificate effectively begins the existence of the corporation as of the date set out on the certificate.

Articles of Incorporation may be submitted by one or more persons who must be 18 years of age or over, and not of unsound mind or bankrupt, or by another corporation.

A corporation must also have one or more directors who must be 18 years of age or over and not be disqualified by the provisions of the act.

The CPPSB provides instructions for submitting Articles of Incorporation. The forms may be obtained from a local stationer or they come as part of a package that may be purchased at nominal cost from the publisher (see order form at front of book). Sample 9 is a copy of the Articles of Incorporation for a service corporation — in this case, a personnel agency having one director. It is incorporated with unlimited share capital provisions and has no special shares.

You will readily see the information that must be supplied with each application. By using this as a guide and supplying your own information, you will be able to complete your own Articles.

Given below is a more detailed discussion of the matters to be considered in completing each individual article. The numbered headings below correspond to the individual articles as they appear on your Articles of Incorporation form.

1. Name

The name of the corporation should have been submitted to a name search firm and a report returned to you. **Note:** The company name must be entered in BLOCK CAPITAL LETTERS under this item.

2. Registered office

The registered office, which is where the registers and records of the corporation must be kept, must be located in Ontario. The registered office can be changed only by following the procedures set out in section 14 of the Business Corporations Act (Ontario).

Give the municipal address of the corporation, including the suite, room, or apartment number, where applicable. If there is no street name or number, use a rural route number. A post office box number is not an acceptable address. The example assumes that the business address of the corporation differs from the residential address of the incorporator or incorporators.

January 7, 200–

Nameless Name Searchers
111 Founders Lane
Anytown, Ontario

Dear Director:

Re: John Doe & Associates Limited   1

       John Doe's Personnel Incorporated   2

       J.D. Personnel Corporation   3

We wish to incorporate under one of the above names, which are listed in order of our preference. Please do the required search and report to us.

Enclosed is a certified cheque for $_____.

Yours truly,

JAD

John A. Doe

---

3.   Number of directors

As mentioned earlier, you may have one or more directors, or set out a minimum and maximum number. The directors are responsible for conducting the affairs of the corporation. Whether your corporation will have one director or many, I recommend that you state the number of directors as a minimum of one and a maximum of, say, ten, to give you the flexibility for change in the future.

4.   First directors

Set out the full names, including first names, initials, and surnames, of the directors together with their address for service, including postal code (which can be a residential, office or other address at which a director can be readily located for service of a document). A post office box number is not a sufficient address. You may change the directors or the number of directors by following the procedure set out in section 125 of the Business Corporations Act (Ontario) and/or in the by-laws of your corporation.

A first director who is not an incorporator must consent to act as a first director by filling out Form 2 under the Business Corporations Act (Ontario) and such consent must accompany the Articles. (See section **e.** of chapter 5, "Shareholders' Resolutions.")

If the corporation has one director, he or she must be a resident Canadian, as defined under the Business Corporations Act (Ontario). If the corporation has two directors, one of the directors must be a resident Canadian. If the corporation has three or more directors, a majority of the directors must be resident Canadians.

SAMPLE 7
NAME SEARCH FORM

ONTARIO NAME SEARCH FORM

DATE: October 3, 200–   SEARCH NO.

AGENT:

☐ Name Search   ☐ Name Reservation

FIRM: THE LAW SHOPPE   979-0000

REQUESTED BY: LORRAINE   TORONTO

Proposed Name: CLARI   ICE CREAM & CANDY LTD.

Nature of Business: _____

Derivation of Key Word
☐ Coined Word   ☐ Person's Name   ☐ Place Name
☐ Dictionary Word   ☐ Foreign Word Language & Meaning: _____

Consent of other _____

Individual, body _____

corporate or firm _____

Proposed Name
☐ Incorporation with Capital   ☐ Extra Provincial Licence   ☐ Charge of Name*
☐ Incorporation without Capital   ☐ _____

   *Give Present Name _____

Reservation   ☐ Please Reserve if Cleared

Second Choice: HARMONY ICE CREAM & CANDY LTD.

Third Choice: GIE'S ICE CREAM & CANDY LTD.

PLEASE NOTE: Both this form and the computer printout bearing the Companies and Personal Property Security Branch (CPPSB) clearance stamp, must accompany the articles application. Although we endeavor to ensure accuracy, we cannot assume responsibility for any errors or ommissions.

PLEASE SEE REVERSE SIDE FOR CONDITIONS AND ADDITIONAL REQUIREMENTS

Ontario | Ministry of Consumer and Business Services | Ministère des Services aux consommateurs et aux entreprises | **Registration Form 2**
under the Business Names Act - Corporations
Enregistrement Formule 2
en vertu de la *Loi sur les noms commerciaux (Personnes morales)*

Print clearly in CAPITAL LETTERS /
Écrivez clairement en LETTRES MAJUSCULES

1. Registration Type
Type d'enregistrement

If B, C, or D enter "Business Identification Number" /
En cas de B, C ou D, inscrivez le n° d'identification de l'entreprise.

Page _____ of / de _____

| A ☐ New / Nouvel | B ☒ Renewal / Renouvellement | C ☐ Amendment / Modification | D ☐ Cancellation / Révocation | BIN / NIE Business Identification No./ le n° d'identification de l'entreprise |

2. Business or Identification Name / Nom commercial ou d'identification

JOLLY JOHN'S PERSONNEL SERVICES

3. Mailing Address Adresse postale

| Street No / N° de rue | Street Name / Nom de la rue | Suite No./ Bureau n° |
| 390 | BAY STREET | 5600 |

| City / Town / Ville | Province / Province | Postal Code / Code postal |
| TORONTO | ONTARIO | Z1P 0G0 |

Country / Pays
CANADA

4. Address of principal place of business in Ontario
Adresse de l'établissement principal en Ontario
(P.O. Box not acceptable)
Case postale non acceptable)

☒ Same as above /
comme ci-dessus

| Street No./ N° de rue | Street Name / Nom de la rue | Suite No./ Bureau n° |

| City / Town / Ville | Province / Province | Postal Code/ Code postal |
| | ONTARIO | |

Country / Pays
CANADA

5. Give a brief description of the **ACTIVITY** being carried out under the business/identification name.
Résumez brièvement le genre d'**ACTIVITÉ** exercée sous le nom commercial ou d'identification.
Note: Limit to 40 characters

PROVIDING PERSONNEL SERVICES *

6. Corporation Name
Personne morale

JOLLY JOHN'S PERSONNEL SERVICES INC.

7. Ontario corporation number
Numéro matricule de la personne morale en Ontario

1234567

8. Jurisdiction in which the corporation was incorporated
Le territoire de compétence où la personne morale a été constituée.

ONTARIO

9. Address of Head or Registered Office of the corporation (P.O. Box not acceptable)
Adresse du siège social ou du bureau enregistré de la personne morale. *(Case postale non acceptée)*

| Street No./ N° de rue | Street Name / Nom de la rue | Suite No./ Bureau n° |
| 390 | BAY STREET | 5600 |

| City / Town / Ville | Province / Province | Postal Code/ Code postal |
| TORONTO | ONTARIO | Z1P 0G0 |

Country / Pays
CANADA

10. Print name of person authorizing this registration *(either an officer, or a director, or a person acting under a power of attorney)*
Indiquez en lettres majuscules le nom de la personne autorisant l'enregistrement *(dirigeant, administrateur, ou personne habilitée en vertu d'une procuration).*

| Last Name / Nom de famille | First Name / Prénom | Middle Initial / initiale 2e prénom |
| DOE | JOHN | D. |

If person authorizing the registration is not an individual (eg. corporation, trust, syndicate), print name here and do not complete last, first and middle names above.
Si la personne qui autorise l'enregistrement n'est pas un individu (c'est-à-dire une personne morale, un trust ou syndicat) ne pas remlir le nom de famille, prénom et 2e

Additional Information / Renseignements supplémentaires

MINISTRY USE ONLY - RÉSERVÉ AU MINISTÈRE

07197 (02/2003)

*****Note:** limit to 40 characters.

5. Restrictions

A business incorporated under the Business Corporations Act (Ontario) has the capacity and the rights, powers, and privileges of a natural person. Therefore, there is no need to itemize the objects, or the types of business dealings, that the corporation proposes to carry on.

However, you may wish to restrict the corporation by its Articles to conducting business within certain bounds. If so, you should set out those restrictions in Article 5. For most corporations, it will not be necessary to do so. If you restrict the type of business that the corporation proposes to carry on, it is important to note that any conduct by the corporation outside of the restrictions in the Articles is not necessarily invalid.

6. Class of shares

The Business Corporations Act (Ontario) requires the Articles to include the classes and any maximum number of shares that a corporation is authorized to issue, and if there is more than one class of shares, the conditions for each class.

If no maximum number of shares is specified, the corporation will have an unlimited number of each class of shares that the Articles provide for. A single incorporation fee is payable regardless of the number of authorized shares.

7. Rights, privileges, restrictions, and conditions on each class of share

The Business Corporations Act (Ontario) does not prescribe specific nomenclature for shares. There is no longer a class of common shares; nor is there reference to special or "preference" shares. You only need be concerned with the concept of "shares." If the corporation has only one class of shares, the rights of all shareholders are equal in all ways and include the right to vote at all meetings of shareholders and to receive the remaining property of the corporation upon dissolution.

If the Articles provide for more than one class of shares, the rights in each class must be stated. The right to vote and to receive the remaining property upon dissolution must be attached to at least one class of shares, although both rights need not be attached to the same class.

8. Restrictions, transfer, and ownership of shares

The restrictions and special provisions relating to the allotment, issue, or transfer of shares as set out in the Articles are common for a corporation that is not offering its shares to the public.

The effect of the restrictions is to preserve the status of the corporation as one that does not offer its shares to the public and provides the directors with a measure of control over the transfer of shares.

You may also wish to restrict the ownership of any class of shares to enable the corporation to achieve the status of a Canadian corporation for certain legislative purposes, and accordingly may set out this restriction on ownership in Article 8.

As mentioned, you may choose one of the clauses listed or draft your own.

9. Special provisions

The two special provisions included in the Articles are to ensure that the corporation falls within the definition of the term "private company" as set out in the Ontario Securities Act and is, therefore, able to issue its shares without filing a prospectus.

10. Names of incorporators

List the full names and addresses of the incorporators. The Articles form must also be signed by all of the incorporators.

g. CONSENT TO ACT AS A DIRECTOR

If a person is named as a director who has not signed as an incorporator, his or her consent to act as director must accompany the Articles. The consent form is included with the package kit available from the publisher.

See Sample 10 for an example of a Consent to Act as First Director.

h. CONSENT BY INDIVIDUAL

If the name of the corporation is the same as or includes that of an individual, he or she should file a consent to the use of his or her name together with a statement that he or she has or will have a financial interest in the corporation. (See Sample 11.)

i. CONSENT TO USE OF NAME OF PARTNERSHIP OR PROPRIETORSHIP

If the corporation is taking over an existing proprietorship or partnership having a name similar to the name proposed for the corporation, a consent signed by the sole proprietor or all partners in the partnership, as the case may be, should be filed with the application, together with an undertaking by the proprietor or partnership to the effect that within six months he, she, or they will discontinue business or change the name to a dissimilar one.

A statutory declaration by the sole proprietor or one of the partners, as the case may be, to the effect that he or she is the sole proprietor or that the consent and undertaking to discontinue doing business under that name has been signed by all partners, must accompany the application.

An example of a consent and undertaking form is shown in Sample 12.

j. CONSENT TO USE OF NAME SIMILAR TO EXISTING CORPORATION

If a corporation is assuming a name that is the same as or similar to an existing corporation, a consent signed by the officers of that corporation should be filed with the Articles together with an undertaking by that corporation that it will dissolve within six months or change its name to one that is dissimilar.

A consent form is shown in Sample 13. It is the same form as used for a partnership.

k. FILING THE APPLICATION

When the Articles of Incorporation are complete, they should be mailed or delivered to the CPPSB at 393 University Avenue, Toronto, together with the incorporation fee which, at the time of printing, is $360. A covering letter (see Sample 14) should also be sent. As earlier provided, Articles of Incorporation may also be electronically submitted by an authorized service provider.

All cheques sent to the CPPSB must be made payable to the "Minister of Finance." Make sure that you write the name of the corporation on the front of your cheque. If all the documents submitted are in order, the CPPSB will stamp your Articles and return them to you. (See Sample 15.)

l. THE BUSINESS NAMES ACT: PENALTIES

The Business Names Act (Ontario) provides in part that no corporation shall carry on business or identify itself to the public under a name other than its corporate name unless the name is registered by that corporation (see Sample 8).

Once filed, a business name registration is valid for a period of five years. At the time of expiry, a registration may be renewed for a further five-year period, in order to maintain use of the name.

If there is a change in the information set out in a registration, you must file an amended registration showing the change within 15 days after the change takes effect.

A corporation carrying on business under a registered name or identifying itself to the public under a registered name must set out both the registered name and its corporate name in all contracts, invoices, negotiable instruments, and orders involving goods or services issued or made by the corporation.

If you fail to register, renew, or amend your business name registration, your corporation cannot maintain a proceeding in a court in Ontario in connection with the corporation's business, except with the permission of the court. However, no contract is void or voidable by reason only that it was entered into by a corporation which was in contravention of the Business Names Act (Ontario) or the regulations at the time the contract was made.

Under the Business Names Act (Ontario) there are significant monetary penalties for corporations that fail to comply with the business name registration requirement. If a corporation fails to file as required by the act, a fine of up to $25 000 can be charged on conviction. If a corporation is guilty of an offence, every director or officer of the corporation and every person acting as its representative in Ontario who authorized, permitted, or acquiesced in such an offence is also guilty of an offence and liable to a fine of not more than $2 000 on conviction.

The Business Names Act (Ontario) provides that a person who suffers damages by reason of the registration of a business name that is the same or deceptively similar to another person's registered name is entitled to recover compensation from the registrant. Compensation is limited to the greater of $500 and the actual amount of damages incurred. In addition, if the person seeking damages is awarded compensation, the court will order the Registrar to cancel the registration that was the cause of the action.

SAMPLE 9
ARTICLES OF INCORPORATION

1

For Ministry Use Only *A l'usage exclusif du ministère*	Ontario Corporation Number *Numéro de la société en Ontario*

ARTICLES OF INCORPORATION
STATUTS CONSTITUTIFS

Form 1
Business
Corporations
Act

*Formule 1
Loi sur les
sociétés par
actions*

1. The name of the corporation is: (Set out in BLOCK CAPITAL LETTERS)
   Dénomination sociale de la société: (Écrire en LETTRES MAJUSCULES SEULEMENT)

J	O	H	N		D	O	E		&		A	S	S	O	C	I	A	T	E	S		L	T	D	.				

2. The address of the registered office is:
   Adresse du siège social:

                              123 NEW STREET
   (Street & Number or R.R. Number & if Multi-Office Building give Room No.)
   (Rue et numéro ou numéro de la R.R. et, s'il s'agit d'un édifice à bureaux, numéro du bureau)

   TORONTO, ONTARIO   ONTARIO | M | 1 | X | 2 | R | 4 |
   (Name of Municipality or Post Office)   Postal Code
   (Nom de la municipalité ou du bureau de poste)   *(Code postal)*

3. Number (or minimum and maximum number) of directors is/are: minimum/*minimal*   maximum/*maximal*
   Nombre (ou nombres minimal et maximal) d'administrateurs: ONE (1)   TEN (10)

4. The first director(s) is/are:
   Premier(s) administrateur(s):

First name, middle names and surname *Prénom, autres prénoms et nom de famille*	Address for service, giving Street & No. or R.R. No., Municipality, Province, Country and Postal Code *Domicile élu, y compris la rue et le numéro, le numéro de la R.R. ou le nom de la municipalité, la province, le pays et le code postal*	Resident Canadian? Yes or No *Résident canadien?* *Oui/Non*
JOHN DOE	123 NEW STREET TORONTO, ON M1X 2R4	YES

07116 (01/2002)

SELF-COUNSEL PRESS — CDN–INCGD–ON (1-1)03

2

5. Restrictions, if any, on business the corporation may carry on or on powers the corporation may exercise:
Limites, s'il y a lieu, imposées aux activités commerciales ou aux pouvoirs de la société:

```
NO RESTRICTIONS
```

6. The classes and any maximum number of shares that the corporation is authorized to issue:
Catégories et nombre maximal, s'il y a lieu, d'actions que la société est autorisée à émettre:

```
AN UNLIMITED NUMBER OF COMMON SHARES
```

07116 (01/2002)

SELF-COUNSEL PRESS — CDN–INCGD–ON (1-2)03

7. Rights, privileges, restrictions and conditions (if any) attaching to each class of shares and directors authority with respect to any class of shares which may be issued in series:
    Droits, privilèges, restrictions et conditions, s'il y a lieu, rattachés à chèque catégorie d'actions et pouvoirs des administrateurs relatifs à chèque catégorie d'actions qui peut être émise en série:

    NONE

SELF-COUNSEL PRESS — CDN–INCGD–ON (1-3)03

4

8. The issue, transfer or ownership of shares is/is not restricted and the restrictions (if any) are as follows:
    L'émission, le transfert ou la propriété d'actions est/n'est pas restreint. Les restrictions, s'il y a lieu, sont les suivantes:

    No share of the corporation shall be transferred without either:
    (a) the express approval of the Board of Directors evidenced by a
    resolution passed at a meeting of directors by the affirmative vote
    of not less than a majority of the directors or by instrument or
    instruments in writing signed by <u>all</u> of the directors; or

    (b) the express approval of the shareholders of the corporation
    expressed by a resolution passed at a meeting of the holders of such
    shares or by an instrument or instruments in writing signed by the
    holders <u>of all</u> of the shares.

SELF-COUNSEL PRESS — CDN–INCGD–ON (1-4)03

07116 (01/2002)

5

9. Other provisions, if any:
   Autres dispositions, s'il y a lieu:

1.   The outstanding securities of the Corporation may be beneficially owned, directly or indirectly, by not more than 35 persons or companies, exclusive of:

(i)   persons or companies that are, or at the time they last acquired securities of the Corporation were, accredited investors as such term is defined in the Ontario Securities Commission (OSC) Rule 45-501 Exempt Distributions as amended from time to time; and

(ii) current or former directors, officers, or employees of the Corporation or an affiliated entity of the Corporation, or current or former consultants as defined in OSC Rule 45-503 Trades to Employees, Executives and Consultants as amended from time to time, who in each case beneficially own only securities of the Corporation that were issued as compensation by, or under an incentive plan of, the Corporation or an affiliated entity of the Corporation;

provided that:

A.   two or more persons who are the joint registered holders of one or more securities of the Corporation are counted as one beneficial owner of those securities; and

B.   a corporation, partnership, trust, or other entity is counted as one beneficial owner of securities of the Corporation unless the entity has been created or is being used primarily for the purpose of acquiring or holding securities of the Corporation, in which event each beneficial owner of an equity interest in the entity or each beneficiary of the entity, as the case may be, is counted as a separate beneficial owner of those securities of the Corporation.

The Corporation has a lien on a share registered in the name of a shareholder or his legal representative for a debt of that shareholder to the Corporation.

And if appropriate:

2.   The Corporation has a lien on a share registered in the name of a shareholder or his legal representative for debt of that shareholder to the Corporation.

07116 (01/2002)

SELF-COUNSEL PRESS — CDN–INCGD–ON (1-5)03

6

10. The name and addresses of the incorporators are:
    Nom et adresse des fondateurs:

First name, middle names and surname or corporate name *Prénom, autres prénoms et nom de famille ou dénomination sociale*	Full address for service or address of registered office or of principal place of business giving street & No. or R.R. No., municipality and postal code *Domicile élu au complet, adresse du siège social ou adresse de l'établissement principal, y compris la rue et le numéro ou le numéro de la R.R., le nom de la municipalité et le code postal*
JOHN DOE	123 NEW STREET TORONTO, ON M1X 2R4

These articles are signed in duplicate.
Les présents statuts sont signés en double exemplaire.

Signatures of Incorporator(s) /
Signatures des fondateurs

JAD
JOHN DOE

07116(01/2002)

SAMPLE 10
CONSENT TO ACT AS FIRST DIRECTOR

CONSENT TO ACT AS A FIRST DIRECTOR
CONSENTEMENT DU PREMIER ADMINISTRATEUR

I, /Je soussigné(e),_____Frederick Evan Folio_____

(First name, middle names and surname)
(Prénom, autres prénoms et nom de famille)

address for service/
domicile élu

_____28 Main Street, Suite 15, Toronto, Ontario, Z1P 0G0_____

(Street & No. or R.R. No., Municipality, Province, Country & Postal Code)
(Rue et numéro ou numéro de la R.R., nom de la municipalité, province, pays et code postal)

hereby consent to act as a first director of
accepte par la présente de devenir premier administrateur de

_____John Doe & Associates Ltd._____

(Name of Corporation)
(Dénomination sociale de la société)

_____Fe Folio_____

(Signature of the Consenting Person)
(Signature de l'acceptant)

CONSENT BY INDIVIDUAL

TO: Companies and Personal Property Security Branch
Ministry of Consumer and Business Services
393 University Avenue, Suite 200
Toronto, Ontario
M5G 2M2

1.   John Doe
(name of consenting individual; or personal representative)

111 Seal Avenue, Toronto, Ontario Z1P 0G0
(street address including municipality & postal code)

HEREBY CONSENTS TO THE FOLLOWING NAME FOR USE BY A CORPORATION:

John Doe & Associates Ltd.
(proposed name of corporation)

2. THE INDIVIDUAL NOTED ABOVE HAS, HAD, OR WILL HAVE A MATERIAL INTEREST IN THE CORPORATION

DATED the 7th day of January, 200– .

JAD
(Signature of individual)

on behalf of: John Doe
(Insert name of individual)

SAMPLE 12
CONSENT AND UNDERTAKING
(By partnership)

CONSENT AND UNDERTAKING BY BODY CORPORATE, PARTNERSHIP, TRUST, ASSOCIATION, ETC.

TO: Companies and Personal Property Security Branch
Ministry of Consumer and Business Services
393 University Avenue, Suite 200
Toronto, Ontario
M5G 2M2

1.   John Doe & Associates Inc.
                    (name of consenting body corporate, partnership, etc.)

    111 Seal Avenue, Toronto, Ontario Z1P 0G0
                  (street address including municipality & postal code)

HEREBY CONSENTS TO THE FOLLOWING NAME FOR USE BY A CORPORATION:

    John Doe & Associates Ltd.
                    (proposed name of corporation)

2.   John Doe & Associates Inc.
        (name of consenting body corporate, partnership, trust, association, etc.)

AND FURTHER UNDERTAKES TO DISSOLVE FORTHWITH OR TO CHANGE ITS NAME TO SOME DISSIMILAR NAME BEFORE THE SAID CORPORATION PROPOSING TO USE THE NAME COMMENCES TO USE IT.

DATED the 7th day of January, 200–   .

                                 John Doe & Associates Inc.
                                    (Name of Corporation)

        By: *JAD*
                            (Signature)

                                   President
                                    (Title of official)

CONSENT AND UNDERTAKING BY BODY CORPORATE, PARTNERSHIP, TRUST, ASSOCIATION, ETC.

TO: Companies and Personal Property Security Branch
Ministry of Consumer and Business Services
393 University Avenue, Suite 200
Toronto, Ontario
M5G 2M2

1.   John Doe & Associates
(name of consenting body corporate, partnership, etc.)

111 Seal Avenue, Toronto, Ontario Z1P 0G0
(street address including municipality & postal code)

HEREBY CONSENTS TO THE FOLLOWING NAME FOR USE BY A CORPORATION:

John Doe & Associates Ltd.
(proposed name of corporation)

2.   John Doe & Associates
(name of consenting body corporate, partnership, trust, association, etc.)

AND FURTHER UNDERTAKES TO DISSOLVE FORTHWITH OR TO CHANGE ITS NAME TO SOME DISSIMILAR NAME BEFORE THE SAID CORPORATION PROPOSING TO USE THE NAME COMMENCES TO USE IT.

DATED the 7th day of January, 200– .

John Doe & Associates
(Name of Corporation)

Per: *JAD*
(Partner/President)

Companies and Personal Property Security Branch
Ministry of Consumer and Business Services
393 University Avenue, Suite 200
Toronto, Ontario
M5G 2M2

Dear Minister:

Re: Incorporation of John Doe & Associates Ltd.

Enclosed please find:

1. Executed Articles of Incorporation in duplicate for the above-named proposed corporation with the necessary consent forms (if applicable).

2. Name search forms

3. Certified cheque in the amount of $360 payable to the Minister of Finance.

Kindly attend to the incorporation of the above-mentioned corporation and return Certificate of Incorporation.

Yours truly,

JAD

John A. Doe

SAMPLE 15
STAMPED ARTICLES OF INCORPORATION

Ontario Corporation Number
Numéro de la société en Ontario

Ontario Ministry of Consumer and Commercial Relations | Ministère de la Consommation et du Commerce

C E R T I F I C A T E
This is to certify that these articles are effective on

SEPTEMBER 30, 200-

C E R T I F I C A T
Ceci devrait certifier que les articles sont efficaces sur

30 SEPTEMBRE, 200-

Form 1
Business
Corporations
Act

*Formule 1
Loi sur les
sociétés par
actions*

ARTICLES OF INCORPORATION
STATUTS CONSTITUTIFS

1. The name of the corporation is: (Set out in BLOCK CAPITAL LETTERS)
Dénomination sociale de la société: (Écrire en LETTRES MAJUSCULES SEULEMENT)

J	O	H	N		D	O	E		&		A	S	S	O	C	I	A	T	E	S		L	T	D	.			

2. The address of the registered office is:
Adresse du siège social:

123 NEW STREET

(Street & Number or R.R. Number & if Multi-Office Building give Room No.)
(Rue et numéro ou numéro de la R.R. et, s'il s'agit d'un édifice à bureaux, numéro du bureau)

TORONTO, ONTARIO | ONTARIO | M 1 X 2 R 4
(Name of Municipality or Post Office) | | Postal Code
(Nom de la municipalité ou du bureau de poste) | | *(Code postal)*

3. Number (or minimum and maximum number) of directors is/are:
Nombre (ou nombres minimal et maximal) d'administrateurs:

minimum/*minimal*: ONE (1) maximum/*maximal*: TEN (10)

4. The first director(s) is/are:
Premier(s) administrateur(s):

First name, middle names and surname
Prénom, autres prénoms et nom de famille

First director	Address for service, giving Street & No. or R.R. No., Municipality, Province, Country and Postal Code *Domicile élu, y compris la rue et le numéro, le numéro de la R.R. ou le nom de la municipalite, la province, le pays et le code postal*	Resident Canadian? Yes or No *Résident canadien? Oui/Non*
JOHN DOE	123 NEW STREET TORONTO, ON M1X 2R4	YES

07116 (01/2002)

SELF-COUNSEL PRESS — CDN–INCGD–ON (1-1)03

4
COMPLYING WITH GOVERNMENT REGULATIONS

a. WHAT OTHER LICENCES AND PERMITS DO YOU NEED?

There are certain government licences and regulations that will affect you and your business. Listed below is a summary of the things you need to know to keep you and your business in good standing with the various governments.

Books and records of your corporation may be audited by federal and provincial agencies from time to time. Therefore, you might as well establish an orderly records and accounts system that will be readily accessible from the beginning. To do this you will need the help of a good accountant who is familiar with small businesses.

The best way to find someone is to ask your successful business friends, people who you admire in a business sense, to supply you with names. Then talk to at least three of them before making a choice.

If you want to learn something about accounting before you talk to an accountant so you can ask some intelligent questions, you might want to refer to *Bookkeepers' Boot Camp: Get a Grip on Accounting Basics*, another title in the Self-Counsel Series, for a simplified explanation of the accounting process.

You can expect to have your books examined by the following government departments: the Workplace Safety and Insurance Board, Canada Customs and Revenue Agency — Taxation (for payroll auditing of employment insurance premiums, Canada Pension Plan contributions, and income tax deductions at source), and Canada Customs and Revenue Agency — Customs and Excise (for the goods and services tax).

The Ontario Corporations Tax Branch will be concerned with your corporation taxes at the provincial level.

You must keep your books and records, including supporting documents, such as sales and purchase invoices, contracts, bank statements, and cancelled cheques, in an orderly manner at your place of business or designated records office.

Canada Customs and Revenue Agency — Taxation requires that you keep all business records and supporting documents until you request and obtain written permission from the department to dispose of them. If you wish to destroy company books or records, you must apply in writing to the director of the district taxation office in your area.

You must also provide detailed information identifying the material and the fiscal period covered by such books.

Note: Some records must be kept indefinitely. These include the minute book, share records, general and private ledger sheets, special contracts and agreements, and the general journal if it is essential to the understanding of the general ledger entries. Other books must be kept until a tax audit or payroll audit has been completed or until at least four years after the taxation year covered, and at that time permission to destroy the records may be given.

b. FEDERAL REQUIREMENTS AND REGULATIONS

1. Goods and services tax

The goods and services tax (GST) is a form of value-added tax imposed by the federal government. Under the GST, a business collects tax from all its customers. The tax is calculated as 7 percent of the sale price of the goods or services.

Each business is entitled to claim a credit for any tax paid on the purchase of goods or services used in its own business. This credit (an "input tax credit") is available to each business in the production and distribution chain except the final non-business consumer of the good or service. The final consumer, therefore, bears the full burden of the tax.

The total amount of GST collected in a given period, typically quarterly, less the input tax credits for that period, must be remitted to Canada Customs and Revenue Agency. If, in any given period, the input tax credit exceeds the tax collected on sales, a business will be entitled to a refund equal to the difference.

All businesses whose gross sales in the preceding year exceeded $30 000, are required to register with Canada Customs and Revenue Agency — Customs and Excise for purposes of collecting and remitting GST on their sales. If a business's gross sales fall below the $30 000 threshold, registration is optional.

Unregistered businesses fall outside the GST net. They are not required to charge GST on their sales but they are also unable to recover GST paid on their purchases. Therefore, even if sales are under $30 000, you should consider registering your corporation.

In order to claim the input tax credit, your corporation must keep detailed records of all GST charges made to it. It is very important to understand how to "track" all of your expenses and what adjustments to your accounting systems may be required. There are also a number of exceptions to the general tax rules that may affect your business.

2. Federal excise tax

An excise tax, in addition to the goods and services tax, is imposed on certain specific goods, whether manufactured or produced in Canada or imported into Canada. The list of excisable items includes, among other things, jewellery, matches, cigarettes, and tobacco.

Complete details can be found in the Excise Tax Act, a copy of which may be ordered from the Canadian Government Publications Centre, Supply and Services Canada, Hull, Quebec, K1A 0S9. Some bookstores also carry copies of the act.

Canada Customs and Revenue Agency — Customs and Excise requires that all persons or firms manufacturing or producing goods subject to an excise tax must operate under a manufacturer's excise tax licence, which can be obtained from the regional or district Excise Tax Office, Canada Customs and Revenue Agency, in the area in which you or your corporation proposes to operate.

Manufacturers licensed for excise tax purposes may purchase or import, free from excise tax, goods that are to be incorporated into and form a constituent or component part of an article or product that is subject to an excise tax, provided they quote their excise tax licence number and relevant certificate.

3. Customs duties

Any business that imports products from abroad must be aware of customs duties, which are levied against goods upon entry into Canada.

There are regulations concerning invoicing, classification of goods, rates of duty and reductions, and exemptions for special classes of articles. It is advisable for you to obtain a ruling on the classification, rate of duty, and valuation prior to commencing shipments.

Foreign exporters and Canadian importers are advised to approach the regional collector of customs, Canada Customs and Revenue Agency, having jurisdiction over the Canadian port of entry for the majority of their goods.

4. Federal income tax

The federal government levies both personal and corporate income tax on monies earned in Canada. Income taxes are applied on income received or receivable during the taxation year from all sources inside and outside Canada, less certain deductions.

Individuals and branches of foreign companies carrying on business in Canada are also liable for income taxes on profits derived from these business operations. Small businesses qualify for special tax rates (see chapter 2 on tax advantages for further information).

If you are an employer, you are required to deduct personal income tax from the pay cheques of all employees on a regular basis. You must remit these funds monthly through any branch of a chartered bank or to the Taxation Data Centre, Ottawa, Ontario.

Deduction of employee benefits must be made from the date of commencement of work. The federal income tax regulations outline the rules for allocating income to provinces when individuals earn business income in more than one province.

For specific information about federal income tax, contact the nearest office of Canada Customs and Revenue Agency — Taxation.

5. Employment insurance

In Canada, workers who become unemployed may qualify for employment insurance benefits under a federal government program. The program is administered by Human Resources Development Canada.

With few exceptions, all employment in Canada performed under a contract of service is insurable, and, therefore, subject to employment insurance premium payments by both the employer and the employee.

The employer is required to collect employee's premiums in accordance with the current premium scales. All matters relating to deductions, remittances, and ruling for employment insurance premiums are handled by Canada Customs and Revenue Agency — Taxation.

6. Canada Pension Plan

The Canada Pension Plan is designed to provide a basic retirement pension for working Canadians. Employees between the ages of 18 and 70 in most types of employment are covered by the plan and must contribute.

Types of non-pensionable employment include agriculture, horticulture, fishing, hunting, forestry, logging, or lumbering where the employee earns less than $250 in cash per year.

The employer is responsible for making the deductions from all eligible employees and must match these deductions with similar contributions. A person who is self-employed is responsible for the entire annual contribution to the Canada Pension Plan.

Note: If you are incorporated and pay yourself a wage, as far as the Canada Pension Plan is concerned you are not self-employed. You should deduct the normal amount from your wage and the company will also contribute as the employer.

Canada Customs and Revenue Agency — Taxation can help employers calculate the amount of employment insurance, Canada Pension Plan, and income tax deductions to be made from employees' salaries. When you apply for an account number, they will supply you with charts to calculate the deductions, along with an explanatory book.

The employer must remit these funds through any branch of a chartered bank or the Taxation Data Centre, Ottawa, Ontario.

c. PROVINCIAL GOVERNMENT REQUIREMENTS AND REGULATIONS

1. Ontario Corporations Tax and Annual Returns

To streamline the collection of corporate information, corporations are now able to file a combined CT23 Corporations Tax and Annual Return. The CT23 Corporations Tax Return collects the information required by the Corporation's Tax Act. The Annual Return collects the information required by the Ministry of Consumer and Business Services under the authority of the Corporations Information Act (Ontario).

Generally, every corporation that is incorporated, amalgamated or continued in Ontario under the Business Corporations Act (Ontario) must file an Annual Return. Every foreign corporation which has a licence endorsed under the Extra-Provincial Corporations Act (Ontario) to carry on business in Ontario must file an Annual Return. A Corporation that is incorporated, amalgamated or continued in a Canadian jurisdiction other than Ontario is not required to file an Annual Return. You may be exempt from filing a CT23 for the current taxation year. Please refer to the Guide to the CT23 Corporations Tax and Annual Return, which can be obtained by contacting the Ministry of Finance to determine if your corporation meets all of the criteria required to be exempt.

A corporation with share capital that is required to deliver a CT23 and an Annual Return is required to file the Annual Return within six months after the end of its taxation year. The following methods are available to file a CT23 and Annual Return.

(a) Complete and submit the preprinted paper Annual Return received with an information guide which may be obtained from the Ministry of Finance;

(b) Submit a plain paper Annual Return produced with certified computer software purchased from any one of many companies;

(c) Submit an Annual Return on a disk (Dfile) produced with certified software available from certified vendors; or

(d) Electronic filing of the Annual Return for most corporations is available with the Ministry of Consumer and Business Services using an authorized service provider.

For further information on the CT23 Corporations Tax and Annual Return, please contact the Ministry of Finance at 1-800-263-7965.

2. Licensing

There are certain specific provincial acts containing licensing regulations and requirements that apply to specific businesses.

While it is impossible to list all the provincial acts and the businesses to which they apply, the following is a list of areas that fall under provincial jurisdiction and about which you should be concerned if you operate a business in these areas.

(a) Door-to-door sales, franchises, pyramid schemes

(b) Firms that loan money or are involved in any way with the consumer finance business

(c) Manufacturers (especially regarding labour laws and factory standards)

(d) Anyone who handles or processes food

(e) Anyone who is in the transport (goods or persons) business

(f) Anyone who is dealing with the natural resources, such as forests, minerals, or water

(g) Anyone in the fish processing business

(h) Anyone who is affected by pollution standards

(i) Anyone who does business on provincially owned land, such as parks and beaches

3. Sales tax

Every provincial government, with the exception of the one in Alberta, imposes a "social service" tax. At present in Ontario the sales tax is 8 percent, which is levied on virtually all tangible personal property that is purchased or imported for consumption or use. This tax is collected by the seller from the ultimate consumer who resides in Ontario. If you are going to be buying merchandise for resale, you will need to apply for a provincial tax number. Upon application, a registration certificate assigning a tax number will be issued by the Ontario retail sales tax branch.

This certificate grants exemption from the payment of the tax on merchandise that is purchased for resale purposes or for merchandise that will become part of tangible personal property intended for resale.

4. Power to hold land

Ontario no longer has any requirements for a corporation to obtain a licence in order to hold land. However, a business incorporated in a jurisdiction other than Canada that obtains an extra-provincial licence in Ontario, has the capacity to acquire, purchase, and hold land. This procedure is outlined in chapter 12.

5. The Workplace Safety and Insurance Board

Ontario was one of the first provinces in Canada to establish a means by which all employers insured themselves against claims by injured workers. The board provides compensation to injured employees from a fund paid into by all employers. The size of each employer's payment depends on the nature of the industry that most of the workers are engaged in and the amount of the payroll.

If your proprietorship or partnership already has employees, the Workplace Safety and Insurance Board will be no stranger to you. However, for those of you who have operated as a proprietorship or partnership with no employees, you should know that upon incorporating a one-person corporation, you become an "executive officer" who is exempt by choice *and* an employee. In this event, you should contact the board to find out whether or not the Workplace Safety and Insurance Act applies to your particular industry and situation. If your corporation pays you salary or wages or makes payments pursuant to a contract of employment, you may be classed as an employee and your corporation regarded as an employer.

However, employers, partners, and their spouses who work for the partnership, independent operators, and directors or executive officers or professional corporations can, in many cases, elect whether or not they wish to be covered by the act. If they choose to be covered they must either estimate their earnings at a rate that is reasonable to the board or, in the case of executive officers of corporations, their earnings, subject to the maximum allowed by the act, are the basis for accident fund assessments.

If you employ subcontractors or independent operators to do work for you and they are not covered by the board, you will be responsible for furnishing a payroll statement for the employees of the contractor. The statement will show the money paid into the board on behalf of the contractor's employees.

The fees and assessments are to be borne entirely by the employers; no deductions may be made from the employees' wages to cover assessments.

If you are planning to incorporate and then engage in a business such as logging, mining, manufacturing, or even farming, you should contact the board prior to incorporation to find out what their procedures are and, in cases of "high risk" businesses, take out coverage so that employees of the corporation are covered from day one and you will not be liable for an accident.

Certainly if you are not prepared for Workplace Safety and Insurance Board assessments and filings, they can cause you a lot of grief. For this reason, I suggest that you inquire at your local office immediately after, or before, incorporating. It is highly likely that you will be responsible for some sort of assessment if you operate as a one-person corporation, where you may not have been made liable previously when you did business as a sole proprietor.

Following is a list of Workplace Safety and Insurance Board Offices:

Toronto

Head office:
200 Front Street West
Toronto, ON M5V 3J1
Telephone: (416) 344-1007

Hamilton

120 King Street West
P.O. Box 2099 Station LCDI
Hamilton, ON L8N 4C5
Telephone: (905) 523-1800

Kingston

234 Concession Street Suite 304
Kingston, ON K7K 6W6
Telephone: (613) 237-8840

Kitchener-Waterloo

55 King Street West, 3rd Floor
Kitchener, ON N2G 4W1
Telephone: (519) 576-4130

London

148 Fullarton Street, 7th Floor
London, ON N6A 5P3
Telephone: (519) 663-2331

North Bay

128 McIntyre Street West
North Bay, ON P1B 2Y6
Telephone: (705) 472-5200

Ottawa

99 Metcalfe Street, Suite 700
Ottawa, ON K1P 1E8
Telephone: (613) 237-8840

Sault Ste. Marie

153 Great Northern Road
Sault Ste. Marie, ON P6B 4Y9
Telephone: (705) 942-3002

St. Catharines

301 St. Paul Street, 8th Floor
St. Catharines, ON L2R 7R4
Telephone: (905) 687-8622

Sudbury

30 Cedar Street Fifth Floor
Sudbury, ON P3E 1A4
Telephone: (705) 675-9301

Thunder Bay

1113 Jade Court, Suite 200
Thunder Bay, ON P7B 6V3
Telephone: (807) 343-1710

Timmins

119 Pine Street South Suite 310
Pine Plaza
Timmins, ON P4N 2K3
Telephone: (705) 267-6427

Windsor

2485 Ouellette Avenue
P.O. Box 1617 Station A
Windsor, ON N9A 7B7
Telephone: (519) 972-4254

Registrar of Appeals

The Workplace Safety and Insurance
Board 200 Front Street West
Toronto, ON M4V 3J1
Telephone: (416) 344-1014
Web site: www.wsib.on.ca

d. MUNICIPAL GOVERNMENT REQUIREMENTS AND REGULATIONS YOU SHOULD KNOW ABOUT

1. Licensing

The Municipal Act authorizes municipalities to license all businesses within their boundaries. Incorporated centres issue licences and permits based on local by-laws.

Communities can control aspects of zoning, land use, construction, and renovation for all types of business activities including the licensing of commercial vehicles.

Contact the local city hall or municipal office for information in these areas. In unincorporated areas, contact the nearest government agent or RCMP detachment.

2. Municipal taxes

Municipal governments levy direct taxes on real estate, water consumption, and business premises.

Property taxes are based on the assessed real value of land and improvements.

Annual notices of assessments are sent out with provision for appeal.

Local business taxes are applied directly against the tenant or the business operator. The business tax is generally based on a percentage of the annual rental value, the property assessment, or the size of the premises.

3. Building requirements

All three levels of government have some responsibility for regulating commercial building. Any construction that is proposed must satisfy all the requirements of the three governments.

The city hall or municipal office brings together all the various building codes and inspections making it possible for approval of planned construction to be obtained at the local level.

The municipality controls the type of building you may construct. Municipal building and zoning regulations control the physical structure and the final use of your building. The municipality also has the power to enforce building regulations.

Before beginning the construction or renovation of a structure, you must obtain a building permit from the municipality. To apply, you must submit preliminary sketches for approval and, once these sketches receive approval, submit complete construction drawings that will be examined to ensure that they meet the federal, provincial, and municipal building standards. If approval is given, then you will be issued a building permit.

Once construction has commenced, various stages of the construction must be inspected before the project can continue.

As each municipality controls certain aspects of construction, the requirements vary from one area to another so you should contact the building department of the municipal government office for specific requirements.

e. MISCELLANEOUS INFORMATION YOU SHOULD KNOW ABOUT

1. The metric system

The metric system is simple to use because relationships are in powers of ten. Approximately 90 percent of the world's population is using or converting to the metric system.

It is important that you be aware of what you need to do to comply with the system. For information on how metric conversion may affect your business, contact the provincial Department of Economic Development or contact Measurement Canada at < http://mc.ic.gc.ca>.

2. Weights and measures

Industry Canada is responsible for the approval and initial inspection of all weighing and measuring devices, such as scales and fuel dispensers that are used in trade.

The Weights and Measures Branch must inspect all new trade devices prior to first use. If you acquire used weighing equipment for commercial use, you should notify the Weights and Measures Branch.

Those devices requiring installation before being inspected (e.g., vehicle scales), must be inspected on site when operational. Movable devices may be factory inspected prior to shipping and the department must be notified when this equipment is in place.

Any relocation of the equipment must be reported to the department to ensure that regular inspections can continue to take place.

The period between inspections varies but is usually every two years. You should note that you are responsible for the cost of the initial inspections.

For further information or to arrange for an inspection, contact the nearest Weights and Measures office of Industry Canada.

3. Packaging and labelling

Any prepackaged consumer product, including food and non-food items, is subject to the packaging regulations of Industry Canada.

Prepackaged products require a label that states the product's net quantity. The information must be declared in metric units, and optionally in Canadian units of measure and must appear in French and English. The identity of the product must also be given in both French and English.

The identity and principal place of business of the manufacturer or the person for whom the product was manufactured must appear on the package in either French or English.

In some instances other information may be required. For example, hazardous or dangerous products must be properly marked, according to the Hazardous Products Act.

Textiles must be labelled with the fibre content according to the Textile Labelling Act. This act provides for the mandatory labelling of such textile articles as wearing apparel, fabrics sold by the piece, and household textiles. It also regulates the advertising, sale, and importation of all consumer textile fabric products.

Articles such as jewellery, silverware, optical products, watches, pens, and pencils, which are made wholly or partly of precious metals, are regulated by the Precious Metals Marketing Act.

There are restrictions on the permissible size for packages, and for certain products only specific sizes are allowed. Contact Industry Canada for detailed information regarding packaging.

4. Patents, copyright, trademarks, and industrial designs

The laws concerning patents, copyright, trademarks, and industrial designs are very complicated and you may find professional help useful. Patent and trademark lawyers specialize in these fields and can ensure that you get the maximum protection and benefit. Look in the Yellow Pages or phone your local lawyer referral service to find patent and trademarks agents available to you.

Before you see a lawyer you might find it helpful to call or write to your nearest Industry Canada office. They have free pamphlets concerning trademarks, patents, copyright, and industrial design. These pamphlets will provide a useful introduction to the subject and familiarize you with the terms used.

The various offices of Industry Canada throughout the region can provide information regarding patents, copyrights, trademarks, and industrial designs and can also accept for dating and transmission to Ottawa applications for these various forms of protection of intellectual property.

(a) Patents

A patent is a monopoly granted by the federal government to an inventor to make, use, or sell the subject matter of his or her invention exclusively in Canada. In exchange for full disclosure of the invention, the government will grant the inventor the exclusive right to make, use, or sell the invention in Canada for 20 years from the filing date of the patent application.

Patents are granted for inventions defined as some technological development or improvement that has not previously been patented or made available to the public.

If you wish to apply for a patent, you must make an application to the Commissioner of Patents, Ottawa, Canada. The application must meet all the requirements of the Patent Act and the Patent Rules.

(b) Copyright

Under the Canadian Copyright Act, copyright subsists automatically in every original literary, musical, dramatic, and artistic work when in a *permanent* form; registration is merely proof of ownership. The author must be a citizen, subject, or ordinary resident, of a Berne Convention, Universal Copyright Convention, or World Trade Organization country (which includes Canada).

The author's rights are recognized as existing once he or she has produced the work. This exclusive right lasts for the life of the author and 50 years after the author's death.

In the case of records, discs, and photographs, the term of protection is 50 years from the end of the year of the first making of the original negative or original record, as the case may be, irrespective of the lifespan of the author.

To register a copyright, you must send your application to the Registrar of Copyright in Ottawa on the form prescribed in the Copyright Rules.

Copies of the Copyright Act and Rules can be ordered from the Canadian Government Publications Centre, Hull, Quebec, K1A 0S9.

(c) Trade Marks

The Trade-marks Act governs trade-mark registration in Canada and also provides for the registration of trade marks used in association with services or wares.

Registration, although advisable, is not compulsory; however, a registered trade mark is more easily protected than an unregistered trade mark.

Registration of a trade mark endures for 15 years and is renewable. The Trade-marks Act outlines the types of symbols that can or cannot be registered.

When sending an application for registration of a trade mark, you must include the filing fee of $150. After the application has been allowed, a further fee of $200 is required for registration of the mark.

The application may be submitted by you, the owner of the trade mark, or your authorized agent. The application is submitted to the Registrar of Trade-marks, Industry Canada, Canadian Intellectual Property, Ottawa.

(d) Industrial designs

An industrial design is any original shape, pattern, or ornamentation applied to an article of manufacture. The industrial design must be made by an industrial process.

An industrial design may be registered in Canada if the design is not identical or similar to others registered, and the application for registration is filed within one year of the publication of the design in Canada or elsewhere.

Registration provides you with exclusive right to the design for a period of five years. Registration may be extended for one additional five-year period.

To register a design, you must file a drawing and description with the Registrar of Industrial Design in Ottawa. A search will be made of earlier designs to determine if the design is novel.

Note: Inquiries about copyright, patents, trademarks, and industrial designs should be directed to Industry Canada, Canadian Intellectual Property, Ottawa.

5. Immigration and citizenship

If you are established in business in a foreign country but wish to live and establish a business in Canada, you must contact the Canadian immigration representative in your country.

It is necessary to apply for permanent resident status while still outside Canada. If you satisfy the immigration officer about the feasibility of your business proposal and you meet all other immigration requirements, it is possible that you will receive permanent resident status.

Canadian citizenship is usually not needed for employment in Canada except in certain areas of the civil service and some professions. If you are considering employment, other than on a temporary basis, permanent resident status must be applied for prior to your arrival in Canada.

Full citizenship can be applied for after three years' residence in Canada.

The duty-free entry of effects owned by persons prior to coming to Canada is provided by Canadian customs regulations. Such goods may not be sold or otherwise disposed of within 12 months of entry without payment of duty.

If you plan to bring with you tools or machinery necessary for your business or profession, be sure to make arrangements before you have them shipped. Customs duty and sales tax are applicable to equipment and you should be aware of the requirements.

Further information on the above may be obtained from the nearest Canadian embassy or consulate or by writing to Citizenship and Immigration Canada, Ottawa.

5
POST-INCORPORATION PROCEDURES

When a Certificate of Incorporation is issued, a new legal entity is created. This means it can sue or be sued or can enter into contracts on its own behalf. This chapter outlines the steps to be taken to complete the organization of the corporation and to preserve its status.

a. PURCHASE OF MINUTE BOOK, SEAL, AND SHARE CERTIFICATES

The Business Corporations Act (Ontario), subject to certain exceptions, requires that certain records of the corporation be kept at its registered office or at such other place in Ontario designated by the directors either in a bound or looseleaf book or by means of a mechanical, electronic, or other device. Most self-incorporators do very well with the bound or looseleaf book as a means of recording and collecting all corporate documents.

Records to be kept include the following:

(a) A copy of the Articles of Incorporation, by-laws, and any unanimous shareholders' agreement known to the directors

(b) All minutes of meetings and resolutions of directors, shareholders, and any committee thereof of the corporation

(c) A register of security holders alphabetically indexed in appropriate categories as to shareholders and holders of debt obligations and warrants, together with the particulars of each, pursuant to section 141 of the Business Corporations Act (Ontario).

(d) A register of directors, including names and *residence* addresses, of all current and former directors, with dates of election and ceasing to be directors

(e) Adequate accounting records

(f) A register of share transfers

By adding your Articles of Incorporation, resolutions as passed, and minutes of meetings of directors or shareholders, if held, you can keep your records in one book. You are also required to institute a proper set of financial or accounting records for the corporation.

For the purpose of executing most documents in Ontario, you may (but are not required to) obtain a corporate seal. The seal must be endorsed with the exact name of the corporation as set out in its Articles and for this reason should not be ordered until the Certificate of Incorporation is received.

Minute books containing all the necessary registers may be purchased from the publisher. A seal may also be ordered from the publisher with the order form at the front of the book. The package of forms supplied by the publisher includes share certificates.

b. ORGANIZING THE CORPORATION

1. By-laws and resolutions

By-laws of the corporation are rules that govern its internal affairs. Resolutions are the acts of the shareholders or directors governing the course of the business of the corporation (e.g., you pass a resolution to elect a new director).

The Business Corporations Act (Ontario) provides for the passage of by-laws and resolutions either at meetings of shareholders or directors, as the case may be, or by written consent of all the shareholders or directors. Your way of conducting the corporation's business will depend on the situation you are in.

In small, closely held corporations, it is usually more convenient to pass resolutions and by-laws by written consent. For this reason, details about the notice periods required for calling meetings and who must be present are not discussed here. The post-incorporation procedures set out here are all based on the passage of resolutions and by-laws by the written consent of all shareholders and directors.

You may have ordinary or special resolutions. An ordinary resolution is one that is submitted to a meeting of the shareholders and passed by at least a majority of the votes cast. A special resolution is one submitted to a special meeting of the shareholders duly called for the purpose of considering the resolution, and passed by at least two-thirds of the votes cast or, alternatively, consented to by each shareholder in writing.

Unless otherwise provided by the Articles, the by-laws, or a unanimous shareholders' agreement, the directors may, either with a quorum at a meeting, or unanimously in writing by resolution, enact a by-law that regulates the business or affairs of the corporation, and they shall submit the by-law to the shareholders at the next meeting of shareholders for confirmation or, alternatively, obtain the written consent of the shareholders.

A general by-law can be passed and become effective immediately and continues in effect when confirmed by the shareholders. A resolution must be confirmed by the shareholders before it can become effective.

If a by-law is not confirmed at the annual shareholders' meeting or at a prior meeting of shareholders or in writing by all shareholders entitled to vote, that particular by-law or similar by-law ceases to be effective on the date it was rejected by the shareholders.

Resolutions are valid on the date they are passed by the directors and shareholders and continue to be valid until revoked or changed by resolutions of directors that are either immediately or eventually confirmed by shareholders at the annual general meeting.

2. The general by-law

Sample 16 shows a general by-law designed for use by almost any type or size of corporation. The set shown in the sample is included with the package of incorporation forms available from the publisher.

A lawyer should be consulted if you wish to make any substantive amendments to them. The set, as it will be adopted by your corporation, should be read carefully to ensure that you comply with it in carrying on business.

You adopt the general by-law by having all the shareholders and directors place their signatures at the end on the last page and by setting out the date on which all of the shareholders and directors consented to its adoption.

c. BANKING ARRANGEMENTS

Unless the Articles, general by-law, or the provisions of a unanimous shareholders' agreement provide otherwise, the Articles are deemed to state that the directors may, without authorization of the shareholders, borrow money on the credit of the corporation; issue, reissue, sell, or pledge debt obligations of the corporation; in some circumstances guarantee on behalf of the corporation to secure performance of an obligation of another person; mortgage or otherwise create a security interest in any

SAMPLE 16
A GENERAL BY-LAW

BY-LAW NO. 1
A By-law relating generally to
the transaction of the business and affairs
of

(the "Corporation")

TABLE OF CONTENTS

SELF-COUNSEL PRESS — CDN–INCGD–ON (3-1)03

BY-LAW NO. 1
A By-law relating generally to
the transaction of the business and affairs
of

(the "Corporation")

RESOLVED as a By-law of the Corporation that:

1. **INTERPRETATION**

1.1 **Definitions.** In this By-law and all other By-laws and resolution of the Corporation, unless the context otherwise requires:

(a) the following terms shall have the meanings specified:

    (i) "Act" means the *Business Corporations Act* (Ontario), or any statute that may be substituted therefor including the regulations made thereunder, as amended from time to time;

    (ii) "Articles" means the Articles of Incorporation of the Corporation as amended or restated from time to time;

    (iii) "Board" means the board of directors of the Corporation;

    (iv) "Chairman of the Board" means the Director appointed by the Board from time to time to hold that office;

    (v) "Corporation" means the corporation whose name is set out at the top of this page;

    (vi) "Director" means a member of the Board;

    (vii) "Meeting of the shareholders" means an annual meeting of shareholders or a special meeting of shareholders, or both, and includes a meeting of any class or series of any class of shareholders;

    (viii) "Officer" means an officer of the Corporation;

(b) terms that are defined in the Act are used in this By-law with the same meaning; and

SELF-COUNSEL PRESS — CDN–INCGD–ON (3-2)03

(c)   words importing the singular number shall include the plural number and vice versa, and words importing the masculine gender shall include the feminine and neuter genders.

2.   DIRECTORS AND OFFICERS

2.1   **Number of Directors.** The minimum and maximum number of Directors of the Corporation shall be such as are from time to time set forth in the Articles. The number of Directors within such range shall be determined from time to time by special resolution or, subject to the provisions of the Act, by the Board if so empowered by special resolution.

2.2   **Election and Term.** The Directors shall be elected at each annual meeting of shareholders to hold office until the next annual meeting or until their respective successors are elected or appointed. At any annual meeting every retiring Director shall, if qualified, be eligible for re-election.

2.3   **Quorum.** A majority of the number of Directors from time to time shall constitute a quorum for the transaction of business at any meeting of the Board. If it is necessary to determine the number of Directors constituting a quorum at a time when one or more vacancies exist on the Board, such a determination shall be made as if such vacancies did not exist.

2.4   **Calling of Meetings.** A meeting of the Board may be held at any time upon call by the Board, the Chairman of the Board, the President or any other Officer so empowered by the Board.

2.5   **Place of Meetings.** Each meeting of the Board shall be held at such place within or outside Ontario as may be determined by the person calling the meeting.

2.6   **Notice.** Subject as hereinafter provided, notice of every meeting of the Board shall be given to each Director at least 48 hours prior to the meeting. Notwithstanding the foregoing:

(a)   no notice need be given of the first meeting of the Board subsequent to a meeting of shareholders at which Directors are elected if such Board meeting is held immediately following the meeting of shareholders; and

(b)   the Board may appoint a day or days in any month or months for regular meetings at a place and hour to be named.

SELF-COUNSEL PRESS — CDN–INCGD–ON (3-3)03

A copy of any resolution by the Board fixing the time and place of regular meetings of the Board shall be sent to each Director forthwith after being passed, but no other notice shall be required for any such regular meeting. The accidental failure to give notice of a meeting of the Board to a Director or any error in such notice not affecting the substance thereof shall not invalidate any action taken at the meeting.

2.7   **Votes to Govern.** Every question at a meeting of the Board shall be decided by a majority of the votes cast on the question. In the event of an equality of votes on any question at a meeting of the Board, the Chairman of the Board shall not be entitled to a second or casting vote.

2.8   **Audit, Executive and Other Committees.** Subject to the provisions of the Act, the Board may appoint annually from among its members an Audit Committee and one or more other committees of Directors, including a committee designated as an Executive Committee, and delegate to such committee or committees any of the powers of the Board except those powers which, under the Act, a committee of Directors has no authority to exercise.

Unless otherwise determined by the Board, each committee appointed by the Board shall have the power to fix the quorum for its meetings at not less than a majority of its members, to elect its presiding officer and to fix its rules of procedure.

2.9   **Appointment of Officers.** The Board may from time to time appoint Officers, specify their duties and delegate to them such powers as the Board deems advisable and which are permitted by the Act to be so delegated. The Board may also from time to time appoint persons to serve the Corporation in such positions other than as Officers, with such titles and such powers and duties and for such terms of service, as the Board deems advisable. One person may hold or discharge the functions of more than one officer or other position.

2.10   **Remuneration and Expenses.** Each Director shall be remunerated for his services as a Director at such rate as the Board may from time to time determine. In addition each Director shall be paid such sums in respect of the out-of-pocket expenses incurred by him in attending meetings of the Board, meetings of any committee of the Board of which he is a member, or meetings of shareholders or otherwise incurred by him in connection with the performance of his duties as a Director, as the Board may from time to time determine. Nothing herein contained shall preclude any Director from receiving remuneration for serving the Corporation as an Officer or employee or in any other capacity.

2.11   **Indemnity.** Without limit to the right of the Corporation to indemnify any person to the full extent permitted by law, the Corporation shall indemnify a Director or Officer, a former Director or Officer, or a person who acts or acted at the Corporation's request as a

SELF-COUNSEL PRESS — CDN–INCGD–ON (3-4)03

Director or Officer of a body corporate of which the Corporation is or was a shareholder or creditor, and his heirs and legal representatives, against all costs, charges and expenses, including an amount paid to settle an action or satisfy a judgment, reasonably incurred by him in respect of any civil, criminal or administrative action or proceeding to which he is made a party by reason of being or having been a Director or Officer, or Director or Officer of such body corporate, if

(a)   he acted honestly, and in good faith with a view to the best interests of the Corporation; and

(b)   in the case of a criminal or administrative action or proceeding that is enforced by a monetary penalty, he had reasonable grounds for believing that his conduct was lawful.

3.   SHAREHOLDERS

3.1   Annual and Special Meetings. The Board shall call an annual meeting of shareholders not later than 15 months after the holding of the last preceding annual meeting and may at any time call a special meeting of shareholders.

3.2   Place of Meetings. Each meeting of shareholders shall be held at such place within or outside Ontario as the Board determines.

3.3   Notice of Meetings. Notice of each meeting of shareholders shall be sent not less than 10 days nor more than 50 days before the meeting to each shareholder entitled to vote at the meeting, to each Director, to the auditor of the Corporation and to any other persons who, although not entitled to vote at the meeting, are entitled or required under any provision of the Act, the Articles or any By-law of the Corporation to attend the meeting. The accidental failure to give notice of a meeting of shareholders to any person entitled to notice thereof or any error in such notice not affecting the substance thereof shall not invalidate any action taken at the meeting.

3.4   Persons Entitled to be Present. The only persons entitled to attend a meeting of shareholders shall be those persons entitled to vote thereat, the Directors, Officers and auditor of the Corporation and any other persons who, although not entitled to vote at the meeting, are entitled or required under any provision of the Act, the Articles or any By-law of the Corporation to attend the meeting. Any other person may be admitted to the meeting only on the invitation of the chairman of the meeting or with the consent of the meeting.

SELF-COUNSEL PRESS — CDN–INCGD–ON (3-5)03

3.5 **Quorum.** At any meeting of shareholders, the holders of a majority of the shares entitled to vote at a meeting of shareholders whether present in person or represented by proxy, shall constitute a quorum for the transaction of business.

3.6 **Voting.**

    (a) Voting at any meeting of shareholders shall be by a show of hands except where, either before or after a vote by show of hands, a ballot is required by the chairman of the meeting or is demanded by any person present and entitled to vote at the meeting. On a show of hands, each person present at the meeting and entitled to vote thereat shall, subject to the Act, have one vote. On a ballot, each person present at the meeting and entitled to vote thereat shall, subject to the Act and the Articles, have one vote for each share in respect of which such person is entitled to vote. A ballot so required or demanded shall be taken in such manner as the chairman of the meeting directs.

    (b) Unless otherwise required by the Act or the Articles, every question at a meeting of shareholders shall be decided by a majority of the votes cast on the question. In the event of an equality of votes on any question at a meeting of shareholders either upon a show of hands or upon a ballot, the chairman of the meeting shall not be entitled to a second or casting vote.

    (c) Subject to the Act and the Articles, where, after the date on which a list of shareholders entitled to receive notice of a meeting is prepared in accordance with the Act, a shareholder named in such list transfers any of his shares, the transferee of such shares shall be entitled to vote such shares at the meeting if, at any time before the meeting, the transferee

        (i) produces properly endorsed share certificates, or
        (ii) otherwise establishes that he owns such shares.

3.7 **Representatives.** Upon filing proof of his appointment reasonably sufficient to the chairman of a meeting of shareholders,

    (a) a person who holds shares as a personal representative,

    (b) an individual who has been duly authorized to represent at the meeting a shareholder which is a body corporate or an association, or

    (c) a proxyholder or alternate proxyholder of a personal representative, body corporate or association,

SELF-COUNSEL PRESS — CDN–INCGD–ON (3-6)03

shall be entitled to vote at the meeting in respect of the shares in respect of which such person has been appointed.

3.8　**Joint Shareholders.** Where two or more persons are registered jointly as the holders of shares of the Corporation,

　　(a)　any notice, cheque or other document directed to such persons shall be sent to them at their address as recorded in the Corporation's share register or, if there be more than one address recorded for them in that register, at the first such address;

　　(b)　any one of such persons may give a receipt on behalf of them for a share certificate that is issued in respect of their shares, or for any dividend that is paid in respect of their shares, or for any warrant or other evidence of a right to subscribe for securities of the Corporation that is issued in respect of their shares, or for any evidence of the rights in respect of any conversion, exchange or other change in the share capital of the Corporation that is issued in respect of their shares; and

　　(c)　any one of such persons present in person or represented by proxy at a meeting of shareholders and entitled to vote thereat may in the absence of the other or others, vote their shares as if he were solely entitled thereto, but, if more than one of such persons is so present or represented, they shall vote as one the shares jointly held by them.

For the purposes of this section, several personal representatives of a shareholder in whose names shares of the Corporation are registered shall be deemed to hold such shares jointly.

3.9　**Presiding Officer.** The Chairman of the Board, or a Director designated by him, or failing such designation, a Director designated by the Board, shall preside at a meeting of shareholders. If neither the Chairman of the Board nor any Director is present within thirty minutes after the time appointed for the holding of a meeting of shareholders, the shareholders present shall choose a shareholder then present to be chairman of the meeting.

3.10　**Scrutineers.** At any meeting of shareholders, the chairman of the meeting may appoint one or more persons, who may but need not be shareholders, to serve as scrutineers at the meeting.

3.11　**Dividends.** A dividend payable to any shareholder

(a)   in cash may be paid by cheque payable to the order of the shareholder, or

(b)   in shares may be paid by a share certificate in the name of the shareholder,

and shall be mailed to such shareholder by prepaid ordinary or air mail in a sealed envelope addressed (unless he has directed otherwise) to him at his address as shown in the Corporation's share register. The mailing of such cheque or share certificate, as the case may be, unless in the case of a cheque it is not paid on due presentation, shall discharge the Corporation's liability for the dividend to the extent of the sum or number of shares represented thereby plus the amount of any tax which the Corporation has properly withheld. In the event of the non-receipt of any such dividend cheque or share certificate, the Corporation shall issue to the shareholder a replacement cheque or share certificate, as the case may be, for the same amount or number of shares on such reasonable terms as to indemnity and evidence of non-receipt as the Board, or any Officer or agent designated by the Board, may require.

4.   EXECUTION OF DOCUMENTS

4.1   The Board may from time to time determine the Officers or other persons by whom certificates, contracts or other documents of the Corporation shall be executed and the manner of execution thereof, including the use of printed or facsimile reproductions of any or all signatures and the use of a corporate seal or a printed or facsimile reproduction thereof.

5.   BORROWING

5.1   The Board may from time to time, in such amounts and on such terms as it deems expedient, without authorization of the shareholders:

(a)   borrow money upon the credit of the Corporation;

(b)   issue, reissue, sell or pledge debt obligations of the Corporation;

(c)   except as limited by law, give a guarantee on behalf of the Corporation to secure performance of an obligation of any person; and

(d)   mortgage, hypothecate, pledge or otherwise create a security interest in all or any property of the Corporation, owned or subsequently acquired, to secure any obligation of the Corporation.

SELF-COUNSEL PRESS — CDN–INCGD–ON (3-8)03

The foregoing resolution making By-law No. 1 of the Corporation is passed by all of the Directors of the Corporation pursuant to the *Business Corporations Act* (Ontario).

DATED as of the __15th__ day of _____May_____ 20 0– .

_____   _____
          Charlie Brown   John Doe

_____
          Michael Smith

The foregoing resolution making By-law No. 1 of the Corporation is confirmed without variation by all of the shareholders of the Corporation pursuant to the *Business Corporations Act* (Ontario).

DATED as of the __15th__ day of _____May_____ 20 0– .

_____   _____
          Charlie Brown   Michael Smith

of the corporation's property to secure any obligation of the corporation.

In spite of these inherent borrowing powers, a bank may still require the corporation to pass a borrowing by-law, or execute a borrowing certificate. Your bank manager will supply you with the by-law, resolution, and any other banking papers required to be passed or signed by his or her own bank. The bank will require you to file a copy of the by-law or borrowing certificate with the printed form supplied by the bank.

The original by-law or borrowing certificate should be kept in your minute book and signed as required and the copy should be filed with the bank.

The bank will also require you to file with it a banking resolution on the form supplied by it. This resolution is discussed below. Other forms will be required by your bank, and your bank manager will explain them to you.

You may wish to consider opening an account at a trust company or credit union. Unlike banks, trust companies and credit unions normally pay interest on chequing accounts. However, if you need financing, a bank is probably your best bet because it will lend money on security such as assignment of accounts receivable, whereas trust companies and credit unions will not. They advance loans mainly on mortgages.

In one of the banking forms you will be appointing "signing authorities." These are the persons empowered to write cheques drawn on the corporation. The bank will ask that you name the officers empowered with this responsibility. Usually it is the president alone, or the president and secretary (two signatures required).

You may also want to consider setting up a separate "petty cash" account with wide signing authority (including possibly your secretary) for amounts up to a maximum of $50 or $100. The main account can then be safely protected while at the same time allowing for the smooth operation of the business.

d. DIRECTORS' RESOLUTIONS

After passing the by-law, the directors should pass resolutions (see Sample 17) to accomplish the following:

(a) Appoint officers. Officers of a corporation are appointed by the board of directors to manage day-to-day affairs of the corporation. The directors may designate the offices of the corporation, appoint officers, specify their duties, and delegate powers to them. Two or more offices may be held by the same person. In a one-person corporation, the sole director/shareholder may be responsible for both offices and can function as both president and secretary.

(b) Approve the share certificates. Share certificates are included in the package available from the publisher. You attach one blank share certificate to the minutes of directors, or resolutions of directors, to establish the form of the share certificate of the corporation.

(c) Authorize the issuance of shares pursuant to written subscriptions received from the proposed shareholders.

(d) Adopt the corporate seal. Although a seal is not mandatory, you may still find occasion to affix the corporate seal to various documents and contracts.

(e) Set fiscal year. A corporation is not restricted to a calendar year for the purpose of its yearly financial statements and may choose any year end that is convenient, provided that the first financial year end is within 53 weeks of the incorporation date.

**Resolutions of the Director(s) of
John Doe & Associates Ltd.
(the "Corporation")**

Form and Execution of Share Certificates

BE IT RESOLVED that the form of Share Certificates attached hereto for the Common and Preference Shares be and the same are hereby approved and adopted as the form of share certificates for Common and Preference Shares in the capital of the corporation and that share certificates shall be signed by the President and the Secretary, and the corporate seal of the Corporation affixed thereto by the said officers.

Allotment of Shares

BE IT RESOLVED:

1. 100 shares of the Corporation are hereby allotted to John Doe subject to payment therefor in the aggregate amount of $100.00.

2. The board of directors hereby fixes the sum of $100.00 as the aggregate consideration for the issuance of the said 100 shares.

3. Upon receipt by the Corporation of payment in full for the said 100 shares, they shall be issued as fully paid and non-assessable and certificates therefor be issued to John Doe or as he may in writing direct.

Appointment of Officers

BE IT RESOLVED that the following persons be and they are hereby appointed officers of the Corporation to hold office during the pleasure of the Board, namely:

President - John Albert Doe

Secretary - John Albert Doe

Adoption of Corporate Seal

BE IT RESOLVED that the seal, an impression of which appears in the margin hereof, is hereby adopted as the corporate seal of the Corporation.

(Note: Press your seal on the side of the page beside this resolution.)

Financial Year

BE IT RESOLVED that the first financial period of the Corporation shall terminate on the 31st day of January, (year) and that thereafter the financial year of the Corporation shall terminate on the 31st day of January in each year.

Transfer of Assets

BE IT RESOLVED that the Corporation purchase the motor vehicle, namely a 1998 Chevrolet, serial number 1234567B89, from John A. Doe, shareholder-director, and that the said purchase be secured by a promissory note.

BE IT RESOLVED that the corporation execute the said promissory note in such manner as required to give full effect to the transactions hereinbefore described.

Appointment of Bank

BE IT RESOLVED that the directors open and maintain a bank account in the corporate name at the Canadian Imperial Bank of Commerce, Yonge & St. Clair Branch, and that a copy of the resolution as to signing officers of the company be annexed to these resolutions and the same be adopted as a resolution of the director(s).

The foregoing resolutions are hereby passed by and consented to by the signature of the sole (all) director(s) of the Corporation pursuant to the Business Corporations Act (Ontario).

Dated the _____ day of _____, (year).

JAD

_____
John Albert Doe

(f) Appoint a banker and pass a resolution respecting signing officers and signing authority on the bank account.

e. SHAREHOLDERS' RESOLUTIONS

Subject to the exception set out in the next paragraphs, the Business Corporations Act (Ontario) directs that auditors must be appointed by the shareholders of the corporation. Generally speaking, the auditors are appointed to inspect or audit the books of the corporation to protect the shareholders' interest. Remember that an auditor is a person who is responsible for matching cheques, bills, and receipts with entries in the corporation's books to ensure that everything is done honestly. Your regular day-to-day bookkeeper or accountant would not be called your auditor.

The Business Corporations Act (Ontario) also recognizes that an audit is unnecessary in certain corporations. If the corporation does not offer its securities to the public, all the shareholders may consent in writing to exempt the corporation from the audit provisions of the Business Corporations Act (Ontario). This written consent must be given each year by the shareholders, usually at the annual general meeting, or in the resolutions passed in lieu of the meeting. Most companies will hire an accountant to give advice on the day-to-day running of the business, but these people need not be appointed in the directors' minutes or approved by the shareholders.

Samples 18 and 19 show two alternative resolutions relating to the appointment or non-appointment of auditors.

SAMPLE 18
SHAREHOLDERS' RESOLUTION APPOINTING ACCOUNTANT

Resolution of the Sole Shareholder of
John Doe & Associates Ltd.
(the "Corporation")

Appointment of Accountant

BE IT RESOLVED that MR. CHARLES BROWN, CA, be and he is hereby appointed accountant of the Corporation to hold office until the first annual meeting of the shareholders at a remuneration to be fixed by the Board of Directors, the directors being hereby empowered to fix such remuneration.

The foregoing resolution is hereby passed and consented to by the signature of the sole shareholder of the Corporation pursuant to the Business Corporations Act (Ontario).

DATED the 20th day of January, 200–.

JAD
John A. Doe

Waiver of Audit Requirements of
John Doe & Associates Ltd.
(the "Corporation")

WHEREAS the Corporation is not an offering corporation within the meaning of the Business Corporations Act (Ontario) —

THE UNDERSIGNED, being the sole shareholder of the Corporation, consents to the exemption of the Corporation from the provisions of the Business Corporations Act (Ontario) regarding the appointment and duties of an auditor for the financial period ending January 31, 200–.

DATED the 28th day of January, 200–.

ঝAD

John A. Doe

You should see an accountant to ensure that proper financial records are kept and to complete tax and other returns.

You will recall that our model by-law outlines the procedure for the election of and removal of directors. It states that directors shall be elected and removed yearly at the annual meeting but if this is not done it can be done any time at a special meeting of the shareholders called for that purpose. As mentioned, rarely are these meetings actually held, but you should always take care and prepare the proper resolution to be signed by the shareholders (see Sample 20).

f. COMPLETION OF VARIOUS REGISTERS

Following the issue or transfer of any shares, the appropriate registers should be completed to provide a visual summary of the operation. There are several registers involved and filling them out is quite simple.

1. Securities' register

Following the issuance of shares of the corporation to a person who is already a shareholder of the corporation, the securities' register should be completed by listing that person's name, address, and the total number of shares of the corporation then held by that person.

If and when there is a transfer, the previous entry of that person on the register should be ruled out or otherwise indicating that the person is no longer a shareholder and the new shareholder's name and address inserted on the next line.

If shares are issued to a person who was not previously a shareholder of the corporation, his or her name and address should be added to the shareholders' register and the number of shares issued to that person included in the appropriate place.

Resolution of the Shareholders of
John Doe & Associates Ltd.
(the "Corporation")

BE IT RESOLVED that JACK A. DOE be elected to the Board of Directors until the next annual general meeting, or until his resignation or replacement.

The foregoing resolution was passed and consented to by all the shareholders of JOHN DOE & ASSOCIATES LTD. pursuant to the Business Corporations Act (Ontario).

DATED the 28th day of January, 200–.

JAD

John A. Doe

2. Shareholders' ledger

The shareholders' ledger simply provides a chronological breakdown of the acquisition, sale, and particulars of the shares by each shareholder. The information required is simple and straightforward.

3. Stock transfer register

The stock transfer register provides a chronological breakdown of the various transfers of any new stock. It does not record the issue of new stock, but rather keeps track of it after its initial issue.

4. Directors' register

In the directors' register, the name and residence address of each director is entered together with the date he or she is elected.

When the director retires, the retirement date is entered.

5. Officers' register

In the officers' register, the name and address of each officer is entered, together with the

details of the office(s) held, and the date he or she is appointed.

When the officer retires, the retirement date is entered.

g. THE INITIAL RETURN AND NOTICE OF CHANGE

Within 60 days of incorporation, you must file an Initial Return — Form 1 (with accompanying Schedule A), which functions like an annual return in that all the pertinent information concerning the corporation is disclosed on it (see Sample 21). If any of the information contained in the form becomes outdated, you are required to file an amended notice within 15 days of the change.

If any section of the form is not applicable to your situation, put "N/A" or "Not Applicable" in the blanks. Forms that have sections left blank will be returned as incomplete.

No return fee is charged for filing either the Initial Return or Notice of Change. If you have a change in directors at your annual meeting, you may file a Notice of Change showing the new names and addresses.

This form is available from the Ministry of Consumer and Business Services. The ministry will mail you an Initial Notice with your issued Articles of Incorporation. To fill out the form, follow the instructions for each numbered section.

1. Indicate whether you are filing an Initial Return or a Notice of Change and that the corporation filing the Notice is a business corporation.

2. Insert the Ontario corporation number, which appears on the top right corner of your Certificate of Incorporation.

3. Business corporations must indicate if they offer securities for sale within the meaning of the Ontario Securities Act. Since this book deals with corporations that do not offer securities to the public, check "No."

4. Insert the full date of incorporation in numeric format.

5. Insert the name of the corporation, including punctuation and spacing.

6. State the full and complete address of the registered office. This means giving the suite number if the office is located in a multi-suite building, the postal code, and the municipality or post office designation for the area in which the office is located. A post office box number is not acceptable.

7. If the address of the principal place of business is the same as the registered office address, place an X in the box provided. If the address of the principal place of business is different from the registered office in Ontario, complete the full address, using the guidelines set out

in section 6. above. If the address of the principal place of business is not in Ontario, place an X in the "not applicable" box.

8. Specify whether you prefer to receive correspondence from the Companies Branch in English or French.

9. Schedule A must be submitted with your form. Specify the number of schedules you are submitting.

10. The form must be authorized by a director, officer, or other individual having knowledge of the affairs of the corporation. The name of the individual must be indicated in the box provided and an X must be placed in the appropriate box to indicate whether the individual is a director, officer, or other individual having knowledge of the affairs of the corporation. Signatures must be originals, not photocopies.

11. An Initial Return or Notice of Change — Form 1 may also be filed electronically by an authorized service provider. There is a fee for filing a notice in this manner, which at the time of publication of this book is $23.05. This fee is exclusive of any additional professional fee charged by a service provider.

Now move on to complete all applicable items on Schedule A in full, including the Ontario Corporation Number and date of incorporation. Schedule A must report all information pertaining to directors and officers of the corporation and must show all changes that have taken place since the filing of the Initial Return or most recent Notice of Change.

One director/officer section must be completed for each individual who is a director and/or officer of the corporation. For each individual, provide the full name (first and last names and middle name or initials), and his or her address for service.

If the individual is a director, indicate whether he or she is a resident Canadian. Complete the date, in numeric form, when the individual became a director and, in case you are filing a Notice of Change, when the individual ceased to be a director. If the date ceased has been completed, the date that the director was elected must also be completed.

If the individual is also an officer, complete the date when he or she was appointed as an officer under the appropriate titles; "other" includes officers with functions equivalent to president, secretary, treasurer, and general manager.

Finally, insert the date the officer ceased to hold his or her position, if applicable, as well as the date elected to that position.

The completed form must be mailed or delivered to — Ministry of Consumer and Business Services, Compliance Section, Companies Branch, 393 University Avenue, Suite 200, Toronto, ON M5G 2M2.

Sample 21 illustrates a typical Initial Return. You can see how it is to be altered in the event of a Notice of Change.

All incorporation forms that are not supplied by the publisher may be obtained by calling the Companies And Personal Property Security Branch (CPPSB) information office at (416) 314-8880 and asking for the form by name and number. As you can see, the Initial Return or Notice of Change is marked as Form 1.

SAMPLE 21
INITIAL RETURN — FORM 1

Form 1 - Ontario Corporation/Formule 1 - Personnes morales de l'Ontario
Schedule A/Annexe A

For Ministry Use Only
À l'usage du ministère seulement
Page/Page _____ of/de _____

Please type or print all information in block capital letters using black ink.
Priers de dactylographier les renseignements ou de les écrire en caractères d'imprimerie à l'encre noire.

Ontario Corporation Number
Numéro matricule de la personne morale en Ontario

Date of Incorporation or Amalgamation
Date de constitution ou fusion
Year/Année Month/Mois Day/Jour

DIRECTOR / OFFICER INFORMATION - RENSEIGNEMENTS RELATIFS AUX ADMINISTRATEURS/DIRIGEANTS

Full Name and Address for Service/Nom et domicile élu

Last Name/Nom de famille	First Name/Prénom	Middle Names/Autres prénoms
DOE	JOHN	A.

Street Number/Numéro civique	Suite/Bureau
415	204

Street Name/Nom de la rue
EGLINGTON AVENUE

Street Name (cont'd)/Nom de la rue (suite)

City/Town/Ville
TORONTO

Province, State/Province, État	Country/Pays	Postal Code/Code postal
ONTARIO	CANADA	Z1P 0G0

*OTHER TITLES (Please Specify)
*AUTRES TITRES (Veuillez préciser)

Chair / Président du conseil
Chair Person / Président du conseil
Chairman / Président du counseil
Chairwoman / Présidents du conseil
Vice-Chair / Vice-président du conseil
Vice-President / Vice-président
Assistant Secretary / Secrétaire adjoint
Assistant Treasurer / Trésorier adjoint
Chief Manager / Directeur exécutif
Executive Director/ Directeur administratif
Managing Director/ Administrateur délégué
Chief Executive Officer/ Directeur général
Chief Financial Officer/ Agent en chef des finances
Chief Information Officer / Directeur général de l'information
Chief Operating Officer/ Administrateur en chef des opérations
Chief Administrative Officer / Directeur général de l'administration
Comptroller /Contrôleur
Authorized Signing Officer / Signataire autorisé
Other (Untitled)/Autre(sans titre)

*OTHER/AUTRE
Year/Année Month/Mois Day/Jour

Director Information/Renseignements relatifs aux administrateurs

Resident Canadian/ Résident canadien   YES/OUI   x   NO/NON   (Resident Canadian applies to directors of business corporations only.)/
(Résident canadien ne s'applique qu'aux administrateurs de sociétés par actions)

	Year/Année	Month/Mois	Day/Jour			Year/Année	Month/Mois	Day/Jour
Date Elected/ Date d'élection	200-	09	15	Date Ceased/ Date de cessation		200-		

Officer Information/Renseignements relatifs aux dirigeants

	PRESIDENT/PRÉSIDENT Year/Année Month/Mois Day/Jour	SECRETARY/SECRÉTAIRE Year/Année Month/Mois Day/Jour	TREASURER/TRÉSORIER Year/Année Month/Mois Day/Jour	GENERAL MANAGER/ DIRECTEUR GÉNÉRAL Year/Année Month/Mois Day/Jour
Date Appointed/ Date de nomination	200- 09 15	200- 09 15	200- 09 15	200-
Date Ceased/ Date de cessation	200-	200-	200-	200-

DIRECTOR / OFFICER INFORMATION - RENSEIGNEMENTS RELATIFS AUX ADMINISTRATEURS/DIRIGEANTS

Full Name and Address for Service/Nom et domicile élu

Last Name/Nom de famille	First Name/Prénom	Middle Names/Autres prénoms

Street Number/Numéro civique	Suite/Bureau

Street Name/Nom de la rue

(Street Name (cont'd)/Nom de la rue (suite)

City/Town/Ville

Province, State/Province, État	Country/Pays	Postal Code/Code postal

*OTHER TITLES (Please Specify)
*AUTRES TITRES (Veuillez préciser)

Chair / Président du conseil
Chair Person / Président du conseil
Chairman / Président du counseil
Chairwoman / Présidents du conseil
Vice-Chair / Vice-président du conseil
Vice-President / Vice-président
Assistant Secretary / Secrétaire adjoint
Assistant Treasurer / Trésorier adjoint
Chief Manager / Directeur exécutif
Executive Director/ Directeur administratif
Managing Director/ Administrateur délégué
Chief Executive Officer/ Directeur général
Chief Financial Officer/ Agent en chef des finances
Chief Information Officer / Directeur général de l'information
Chief Operating Officer/ Administrateur en chef des opérations
Chief Administrative Officer / Directeur général de l'administration
Comptroller /Contrôleur
Authorized Signing Officer / Signataire autorisé
Other (Untitled)/Autre(sans titre)

*OTHER/AUTRE
Year/Année Month/Mois Day/Jour

Director Information/Renseignements relatifs aux administrateurs

Resident Canadian/ Résident canadien   YES/OUI   NO/NON   (Resident Canadian applies to directors of business corporations only.)/
(Résident canadien ne s'applique qu'aux administrateurs de sociétés par actions)

	Year/Année Month/Mois Day/Jour			Year/Année Month/Mois Day/Jour
Date Elected/ Date d'élection		Date Ceased/ Date de cessation		

Officer Information/Renseignements relatifs aux dirigeants

	PRESIDENT/PRÉSIDENT Year/Année Month/Mois Day/Jour	SECRETARY/SECRÉTAIRE Year/Année Month/Mois Day/Jour	TREASURER/TRÉSORIER Year/Année Month/Mois Day/Jour	GENERAL MANAGER/ DIRECTEUR GÉNÉRAL Year/Année Month/Mois Day/Jour
Date Appointed/ Date de nomination				
Date Ceased/ Date de cessation				

07200 (03/2002)

SELF-COUNSEL PRESS — (2 OF 2)

6
HOW TO ISSUE, CANCEL, AND TRANSFER SHARES

a. INTRODUCTION

The issuing and cancelling of shares following their transfer can be a relatively simple affair because the form of share certificate is already prepared. Be careful, however, to distinguish in your mind between the initial issues out of treasury (i.e., from the unissued "pool") and simple transfers from one person to another where no new shares are issued. Each involves a different operation. Fortunately, the simplest operation comes first.

The following points should be noted regarding shares generally:

(a) For the average small, private corporation a relatively few share certificates will suffice because there are normally only a few shareholders and each share certificate can represent the total number of shares held by each person. (You do not need a separate certificate for each share.)

(b) Share certificates should, whenever possible, remain with the minute book because if they are sent to the individual shareholder, some will inevitably be lost and you will then be faced with the annoying problem of replacing lost share certificates.

(c) Share certificates have to be issued under the seal of the corporation, when a corporation has a seal, and signed by two officers.

(d) Share certificates should be numbered consecutively in the space provided at the top of the certificate.

(e) You can see the remaining information that is needed by looking closely at the share certificates in Samples 22 and 23.

(f) To cancel shares, simply write the word "cancelled" across the face of the certificate and staple it shut on top of the tab or stub of the certificate (see Sample 23).

(g) You must be sure to follow the procedure outlined in Article 8 of your Articles of Incorporation which will specify the restrictions on the issuing or transferring of shares. For example, if your restriction is that before an allotment or transfer is effective, it must be passed by the majority of the board of directors, then you must prepare the appropriate directors' resolution.

(h) You must be sure that any issue or transfer of shares (also called securities) is made in accordance with the Rules made under the Securities Act (Ontario). Please see section c. in this chapter for further details.

b. SUBSEQUENT ISSUE OF SHARES

The initial issue of shares is usually done during the organization procedure of the corporation and is explained in chapter 5.

The main reason why a small, non-public corporation would want to issue additional shares is to bring in a new "partner." The reasons for this may be either financial or because the new partner is, or will be, a major factor in the running of the business.

Company JOHN DOE ASSOCIATES LTD.

SHARE CERTIFICATE

Certificate # 1

Class Common No. of Shares 10 Par Value none

Registered Name John Doe

Date entered in

Register of Members January 25 200 –

TRANSFER DETAILS

From:

To:

Received (Certificate Number)

this day of , 200 –

NO. 1

10 **SHARES**

INCORPORATED UNDER THE LAW OF THE PROVINCE OF ONTARIO

This is to certify that JOHN DOE AND ASSOCIATES LTD.

is the registered holder of TEN (10)

fully paid and non-assessable Common shares of JOHN DOE AND ASSOCIATES LTD.

with NO par value

Restrictions on Transfer. *There are restrictions on the right to transfer the said shares and a copy of the full text thereof is obtainable on demand and without fee from the Corporation.*

IN WITNESS WHEREOF the Corporation has caused this Certificate to be signed by its duly

authorized officer(s) this 25TH day of JANUARY 20 0 –

John Doe

John Doe

The undersigned, for valuable consideration received, hereby transfers to

_____

(transferee)

_____

(number and class)

share(s) in the authorized capital of the within Company to hold unto the transferee, his heirs, executors, administrators, and assigns, subject to the same conditions on which the transferor held at the time of execution, and the transferee in taking delivery hereof takes the said shares subject to the conditions aforesaid.

DATE_____

SIGNATURE_____

WITNESS_____

Company JOHN DOE ASSOCIATES LTD.

SHARE CERTIFICATE

Certificate # 1   Class Common   No. of Shares 10   Par Value none

Registered Name John Doe

Date entered in

Register of Members   January 25   20 0 –

TRANSFER DETAILS

From:

To:

Received (Certificate Number)

this   day of   , 20 0 –

NO. 1

INCORPORATED UNDER THE LAW OF THE PROVINCE OF ONTARIO

10 SHARES

This is to certify that JOHN DOE AND ASSOCIATES LTD.

is the registered holder of TEN (10)

fully paid and non-assessable Common shares of JOHN DOE AND ASSOCIATES LTD.

with NO par value

CANCELLED

*Restrictions on Transfer. There are restrictions on the right to transfer the said shares
and a copy of the full text thereof is obtainable on demand and without fee from the Corporation.*

IN WITNESS WHEREOF the Corporation has caused this Certificate to be signed by its duly

authorized officer(s) this   25TH   day of   JANUARY   20 0 –

John Doe

John Doe

If the reason for bringing in a new "partner" is to gain management expertise, etc., the major consideration will revolve around who is to control the corporation and have the deciding vote on major issues.

Remember, despite the existence of the corporate entity, it is still very much a partnership in every sense of the word, especially if the shares are to be split equally between two or more shareholders. A "deadlock" between partners may result in either the business being wound up or someone buying out someone else.

The lesson here is to be sure to discuss these potential problem areas before someone is brought in and have an understanding about how the situation will be handled if and when problems develop.

At this point the need for a shareholders' agreement may arise and you will need to consult a lawyer. Such an agreement can provide for the management of the corporation and the division of any of its profits (see chapter 8 for further details).

Without such an agreement, a person holding a minority of the issued shares of the corporation would have no legal or practical way of ensuring that the corporation paid dividends if there were earnings or of ensuring that he or she had some participation in the overall direction of the business of the corporation.

These matters are generally resolved in the form of a shareholders' agreement. It is recommended that the preparation of a shareholders' agreement be referred to a lawyer as there are many complex matters which, if not foreseen and dealt with early in the life of the corporation, may prove unsolvable in later years.

New shares out of the treasury of a corporation can only be issued by a resolution of the board of directors of the corporation. If the board decides to issue new shares in the corporation, it must determine how many shares to issue and the worth for which these shares are to be issued.

If the shares are not issued for money but for assets or past services, the board of directors must specify in its resolution the value of such assets or the value of such past services to the corporation.

Correspondingly, by issuing shares for a value greater than their true value, the average value of every issued share of the corporation increases. Thus, considerable care should be taken by the board of directors in determining the value for which shares of the corporation will be issued.

Sample 24 shows the resolutions of a board of directors issuing shares of the corporation either for money or assets.

c. THE SECURITIES ACT (ONTARIO)

The Securities Act (Ontario) was amended and Rule 45-501 came into force on November 30, 2001. This new Rule eliminates the old "private company" exemption and provides for new prospectus and registration exemptions for the issuance and transfer of securities in Ontario, including an exemption for "closely-held issuers."

To qualify a Corporation as a "closely-held issuer" for the purposes of the Securities Act (Ontario), shares must be subject to restrictions on transfer. The restrictions on the transfer of shares in a Corporation's Articles must meet the requirements of the new Rule in this regard.

In addition to the above, a "closely held" issuer is limited as to the number and type of security holders as follows:

The outstanding securities of the Corporation may be beneficially owned, directly or indirectly, by not more than 35 persons or companies, exclusive of:

(a) persons or companies that are, or at the time they last acquired securities of the Corporation were, accredited investors as such term is defined in the Ontario Securities Commission (OSC) Rule 45-501 Exempt Distributions as amended from time to time; and

(b) current or former directors, officers, or employees of the Corporation or an affiliated entity of the Corporation, or current or former consultants as defined in OSC Rule 45-503 Trades to Employees, Executives and Consultants as amended from time to time, who in each case beneficially own only securities of the Corporation that were issued as compensation by, or under an incentive plan of, a Corporation or an affiliated entity of the Corporation;

provided that:

(i) two of more persons who are the joint registered holders of one or more securities of the Corporation are counted as one beneficial owner of those securities; and

(ii) a corporation, partnership, trust, or other entity is counted as one beneficial owner of securities of the Corporation unless the entity has been created or is being used primarily for the purpose of acquiring or holding securities of the Corporation, in which event each beneficial owner of an equity interest in the entity or each beneficiary of the entity, as the case may be, is counted as a separate beneficial owner of those securities of the Corporation.

If there will never be more than a few shareholders, and those shareholders are resident in Ontario, the issue or transfer of shares is fairly straight forward and can be accomplished pursuant to the steps set out in this chapter. In other circumstances, we recommend that legal advice with respect to any transfer of previously issued securities or the issuance of new securities of a Corporation be obtained. These transfers and issuances are required to be completed in compliance with the provisions of the Securities Act (Ontario) and may, depending on the circumstances of the issuance or transfer, require filings to be made with securities regulators, documents to be delivered to the recipient security holder or legends to be applied to the securities.

d. TRANSFER OF SHARES

As stated earlier, it is important to remember when transferring shares from one person to another (this is not the same as issuing new shares out of treasury) that you follow the requirements set out in Article 8 of your Articles of Incorporation. In other words, whatever restrictions you have on transfer must be noted and the procedure followed as set out.

For example, if your restriction on transfer is that a majority of the board of directors must approve the transfer, a directors' resolution stating this must be prepared (see Sample 25).

As also stated earlier, it is very important to ensure that any transfer complies with Rule 45-501 under the Securities Act (Ontario).

The next step is to physically write the word "cancelled" diagonally across the face of the old certificate, complete the transfer form on the back, including having it signed, dated and witnessed, and then fold it up and staple it to the stub so that the face of it is not conspicuous. This serves to clearly indicate that the share certificate is cancelled and not missing.

Finally, you complete a new certificate in the same manner as the old one, taking care, of course, to insert the new owner's name and new certificate number.

SAMPLE 24
DIRECTORS' RESOLUTIONS TO ISSUE SHARES

Resolutions of the Director(s) of
John Doe & Associates Ltd.
(the "Corporation")

BE IT RESOLVED THAT:

1. Fifty (50) shares of the Corporation (hereinafter called the "common shares") are hereby allotted subject to payment therefor to Jane Doe for $15 000.

2. The Board of Directors hereby fixes the sum of $15 000 as the aggregate consideration for the issuance of the said fifty (50) common shares.

3. Upon receipt by the Corporation of payment in full for the said fifty (50) common shares, the said common shares be issued as fully paid and non-assessable and certificates therefore be issued to the respective allottees, or as they may in writing direct.

OR

WHEREAS the Corporation has agreed with Jane Doe to purchase her 1990 Ford Van truck, registration number XB1234, owned by Jane Doe in consideration of the issuance and allotment of fifty (50) fully paid and non-assessable shares of the Corporation;

RESOLVED THAT:

1. The directors hereby determine a fair market value to be the sum of $5 000 as the consideration for which fifty (50) shares of the Corporation may be allotted and issued.

2. The directors hereby determine by this express resolution that the Ford Van referred to above is in all the circumstances of the transaction the fair equivalent of $5 000.

3. Fifty (50) shares of the Corporation are hereby allotted to Jane Doe.

4. The said shares are issued as fully paid and non-assessable shares and the proper officers of this Corporation are hereby authorized to issue and deliver certificates for such shares to Jane Doe upon receipt by this Corporation of conveyances and transfers of the said vehicle to the Corporation.

The foregoing resolution(s) are hereby passed and consented to by the signature of the director(s) of the Corporation pursuant to the Business Corporations Act (Ontario).

DATED the 25th day of January, 200–.

John A. Doe

DIRECTORS' RESOLUTIONS TO TRANSFER SHARES

Resolutions of the Director(s) of
John Doe & Associates Ltd.
(the "Corporation")

BE IT RESOLVED THAT:

1. Ten (10) shares of the Corporation registered in the name of John Doe and evidenced by share certificate no. 1 be transferred to Jane Doe.

2. Share certificate no. 2 for ten (10) shares be issued to Jane Doe and that the transfer as set out be duly recorded on the share registry of the Corporation.

The foregoing resolutions are hereby passed and consented to by the signature of the director(s) of the Corporation pursuant to the Business Corporations Act (Ontario).

DATED the 25th day of January, 200–.

JAD

John A. Doe

7
TRANSFERRING ASSETS INTO A NEW CORPORATION

Once your business is incorporated and organized, the next step is for your corporation to acquire assets. The assets of your proprietorship or partnership would generally be transferred to the corporation. The assets the new corporation acquires can be purchased in the normal course of business with cash that is in the corporation bank account (e.g., share subscription proceeds or money lent to the corporation by a shareholder or financial institution) or in exchange for debt or shares issued by the corporation to the transferor of the assets.

Transferring assets to the corporation may simplify accounting. For example, it is easier for the corporation to own assets and deduct depreciation and operating expenses rather than have each shareholder own them and rent them to the corporation. Otherwise both the corporation and the shareholders would have to keep records of the assets and corresponding rental payments.

You should remember, however, that after the transfer, the assets become the property of the corporation and are subject to seizure by creditors of the corporation. If you want to minimize your risk of loss, you may transfer certain assets that are necessary for carrying on the business into the corporation and retain other assets, like your car, in your own name and lease them to the corporation. As a result, if the business enterprise fails, these assets would not be subject to seizure.

a. FEDERAL INCOME TAX CONSIDERATIONS

In the absence of certain provisions in the Income Tax Act (Canada), which will be discussed shortly, transfers of property to a person with whom you do not deal at arm's length (like your corporation) are deemed to take place for income tax purposes at fair market value, even though the transfer price may be less than fair market value. This could result in the triggering of a gain (either income or a capital gain) or the recapture of capital cost allowance. If the parties are not dealing at arm's length, the transferor will be deemed to have received proceeds of disposition equal to the fair market value of the property transferred even though no consideration was paid or received, and the transferee will generally be deemed to have acquired the assets at the lesser of fair market value and the amount actually paid.

For example, assume that you purchased a car for $20 000 for your proprietorship, and over a couple of years you depreciated the car for tax purposes down to $12 000. You then incorporate and transfer the car into the corporation at a deemed price of its fair market value of, say, $14 000. Subject to the discussion below, you would have to include $2 000 in your personal income, being the amount of the recaptured capital cost allowance (i.e., tax depreciation).

b. SECTION 85 ROLLOVER

In order to eliminate the onerous tax consequences that have just been described, section 85 of the Income Tax Act (Canada) permits you and the corporation to *elect* for income tax purposes that the transfer take place at a price agreed on by the parties, so that any gain or recapture that would otherwise arise on a transfer at fair market value may be deferred in whole or in part depending on the elected amount. The elected amount becomes the proceeds of disposition of the property to the transferor and the cost of the property to the transferee corporation.

In the example above, the elected amount for the car could be $12 000, which is the depreciated value for tax purposes in the proprietorship's books. Accordingly, there would be no tax consequence to the vendor, and the car would appear on the corporation's books for income tax purposes at $12 000. (If the elected amount was $13 000, you would be required to include $1 000 of recaptured depreciation in your income.)

There are certain requirements in section 85 of the Income Tax Act (Canada) for the transfer of assets into the corporation to occur at an amount other than the fair market value of the assets. These requirements are as follows:

(a) The corporation to which the assets are transferred must be a "taxable Canadian corporation" (a newly incorporated federal or provincial business corporation would qualify). The transferor does not need to be a resident of Canada, and can be an individual, partnership, trust, or other corporation.

(b) The property transferred must be "eligible property." This would include depreciable or non-depreciable capital property, inventory (other than real estate), eligible capital property (e.g., goodwill and trademarks), or resource properties. Real estate that is capital property owned by a non-resident person is not eligible property unless it is used in the year of transfer in a business carried on in Canada by the non-resident person.

(c) The transferor and transferee must make a joint election selecting the transfer price in accordance with the rules described below on a form prescribed by the government and must file the form before the earlier of the due date for the income tax return of the transferor or the corporation for the taxation year in which the transfer occurs, or else a late filing penalty will be levied. If the election is filed more than three years late, the permission of the Minister of National Revenue will be required.

(d) The transferor must receive some share consideration for the transfer (one share of the transferee corporation is enough). The balance of the consideration can be non-share consideration, like cash or a promissory note or other form of security, but to avoid income tax consequences, the amount of the non-share consideration should not be greater than the cost for tax purposes of the item being transferred. To determine the cost for income tax purposes, you should consult your professional advisors.

When determining what amount to elect for the transfer price, the following rules apply:

(a) The elected amount cannot be less than the fair market value of the non-share consideration received by the transferor.

(b) The elected amount cannot exceed the fair market value of the property transferred.

(c) Where the elected amount exceeds the fair market value of the property, the elected amount will be deemed to be the fair market value. Similarly, if the elected amount is less than the fair market value of the non-share consideration received, the elected amount will be deemed to be the amount of the non-share consideration.

(d) More complex rules apply with respect to the transfer of depreciable property or eligible capital property (e.g., goodwill) and professional advice should be sought.

c. PROVINCIAL TAX CONSIDERATIONS

It is equally important to consider the application of Ontario or other provincial retail sales tax to a transaction like the one described above.

The transfer of assets into a newly incorporated corporation is exempt from Ontario retail sales tax if, at the time of the transfer, the transferor wholly owns the corporation (either directly or through another wholly owned corporation), and the assets have not previously been exempted from retail sales tax under a similar rollover, and any retail sales tax in respect of all prior transfers of the property has been paid. (For other provinces, consult your professional advisors.)

In other words, you may transfer assets to a corporation of which you are the sole shareholder free of retail sales tax, provided the assets in question have not previously been transferred relying on this rollover provision (i.e., the rollover is only available once per property). If you try to transfer the same assets in the new corporation to another corporation, Ontario retail sales tax may be payable.

The same situation applies in the case of a partnership provided the partners retain the same proportionate interest in the newly incorporated corporation as they had in the partnership.

Inventory purchased by the corporation for resale is also not subject to retail sales tax. The corporation should obtain a vendor's permit for retail sales tax purposes, if it is reselling goods subject to provincial retail sales tax.

d. GOODS AND SERVICES TAX

The application of the goods and services tax ("GST") to a section 85 transfer must also be considered. Generally, the transfer of assets to a corporation represents a taxable supply, subject to 7 percent GST, unless the supply is an exempt supply or a zero-rated supply.

Therefore, assuming that both parties are registered for GST purposes, the corporation will be required to pay 7 percent GST on the fair market value of the property transferred (and not on the elected amount). The transferor will be required to collect the GST and remit the same amount to the government in accordance with the usual rules. If the asset is used in a commercial activity of the corporation, the corporation will be entitled to an input tax credit for GST purposes in respect of the acquisition.

In certain circumstances, where all or substantially all of the assets of a business, such as a proprietorship or partnership, are being transferred into a corporation under a section 85 transfer, the corporation may be exempt from payment of GST on the transfer. The exemption, if available for the transfer in question, is claimed through filing specific GST tax forms. Consult your tax advisor or accountant about the possible GST exemption for such asset transfers.

Special rules apply where real estate is transferred to the corporation. You should consult your tax advisors about such transfers.

e. COMPLETING THE TRANSFER OF ASSETS

Once you have determined which assets you wish to transfer to the corporation and have considered the possibility of a section 85 election, you should prepare documents to demonstrate that actual title to the assets has passed to the corporation.

For example, where a motor vehicle is being transferred, make sure that the usual government transfer forms are filled out and registered. Also, any car insurance policies should be transferred into the name of the corporation.

You should prepare and execute a bill of sale of the assets transferred and keep it with the minute book of the corporation.

Where accounts receivable are being transferred, all those persons who owed the proprietorship or partnership money should be contacted and informed to make payment to the corporation. (An election under section 22 of the Income Tax Act (Canada) is also available to permit a rollover of reserves in respect of accounts receivable. You should consult your professional advisors concerning this election.)

Finally, the directors of the corporation should pass a resolution authorizing the acquisition of the assets by the corporation and the making of a section 85 election, if appropriate. This resolution should be documented in the minutes.

Since transactions like the one described can be complex, it is recommended that you seek the advice of your accountant and lawyer to ensure that all the steps are completed properly.

f. FINANCING THE TRANSACTION

When an asset is sold to a corporation, it must give something back in return as consideration for the transfer. Under section 85, this must include some share consideration. The share consideration may be combined with non-share consideration, the simplest form of which is a demand promissory note (see Sample 26). Promissory note forms can be picked up at stationery stores or ordered from the publisher.

SAMPLE 26
DEMAND NOTE

$1 999   March 30, 200–

ON DEMAND after date I promise to pay to the order of John Doe of Toronto, Ontario, one thousand nine hundred and ninety-nine dollars ($1 999) with interest at the rate of ten percent (10%) per annum, as well after as before demand, FOR VALUE RECEIVED.

JOHN DOE & ASSOCIATES LTD.

Per:

Seal

JAD
President

A note like this should be executed on behalf of the corporation in favour of each party transferring assets to the corporation if non-share consideration is appropriate under the circumstances.

Under the terms of the note shown in Sample 26, John Doe is entitled to "demand" payment at any time. You may wonder why Mr. Doe would not demand payment immediately of the note.

First, he is not likely to demand payment unless there are sufficient funds in the corporation's bank account to pay him, and he is in the best position to know whether or not he can collect, particularly when in most instances he is the sole shareholder.

Second, the demand note is in effect a form of financing of the corporation by Mr. Doe. Presumably Mr. Doe would not demand payment unless the corporation had a source of funds from which to pay the note and Mr. Doe had an immediate need for the funds.

Thus, the fact that a corporation owes money payable on demand to shareholders of the corporation is not uncommon. Usually an informal agreement between the working shareholders as to where and when the note should be presented for payment is sufficient.

Interest on the note is taxable in the hands of the holder. Interest is also generally deductible to the corporation if the note represents all or part of the price for an asset acquired by the corporation for the purpose of earning income, or if the note evidences borrowed money used by the corporation for the purpose of earning income. Repayment of the principal amount due the holder is not taxable, as it constitutes repayment of a loan made to the corporation.

There is one risk that is taken when transferring assets to a corporation. If the corporation should go bankrupt or have judgments registered against it, the assets may be subject to seizure by the judgment creditor and, in any event, will vest in the bankruptcy trustee. In the case of the debt owed to you by the corporation, it would be relegated to general creditor status and you would share in the proceeds of the re-sale of the corporation's assets along with other creditors.

This happens infrequently because you can usually foresee these events some time before they occur and make demand on your note and collect on it, well enough in advance of the corporation's financial difficulty that the repayment of your promissory note would not be considered a fraudulent preference.

Where there is a transfer of numerous and valuable assets, extra precaution is usually taken in the form of a security agreement between the corporation and the transferor. This elevates the transferor or shareholder to secured creditor status and entitles him or her to a higher ranking if there is a claim on the assets. In this case, it is recommended that a lawyer be consulted as a security agreement needs to be properly drafted and registered to be effective.

8

DO YOU NEED A SHAREHOLDERS' AGREEMENT?

Once your business is incorporated and organized and any licences required by your corporation have been obtained, you are ready to start business. As your business grows, if there is more than one shareholder, you should consider implementing a shareholders' agreement.

A shareholders' agreement is an agreement entered into by some, and generally all, the shareholders of a corporation to establish the course of future conduct in a variety of areas. These may include the following:

(a) The right of a shareholder to nominate a director or directors

(b) The appointment of officers of the corporation

(c) The right of shareholders to compete, or the obligation not to compete, with the corporation

(d) The pro rata right of shareholders to participate in future offerings of the corporation

(e) Restrictions or prohibitions on the transfer of shares

(f) The right or obligation of shareholders or the corporation to purchase the shares of a shareholder upon the occurrence of an event (e.g., irreconcilable differences of opinion or the death or permanent disability of a shareholder), together with a formula for valuation of the shares to be purchased, and the mechanism for purchase

(g) Mechanisms for the resolution of disputes

Of the above features, those most commonly seen in shareholders' agreements are (a), (d), and (e). The remaining features appear with varying frequency, depending on the business involved and the circumstances surrounding the shareholders. In any event, it is important to note that a shareholders' agreement should be drafted as simply as possible. The more complex the agreement the more likely is the possibility of it being unworkable.

Consider, now, the most common features in a shareholders' agreement, and why such provisions are important.

a. RIGHT TO NOMINATE A DIRECTOR

When there is no shareholders' agreement, a corporation is managed by its board of directors, and the board is elected by the shareholders. In small, closely held corporations, where there are only one or two shareholders, the directors are often shareholders as well. This generally assures each person that he or she will be involved in the management. As a result, the shareholders' agreement would not necessarily require the representation of each shareholder on the board since each would be a director.

However, a shareholder having a minority interest in the corporation would want to be assured that he or she, or someone he or she chooses, is a director. This is generally accomplished through an agreement. Otherwise the majority shareholders would be free to select the directors of their choice.

b. PRO RATA RIGHTS AND OBLIGATIONS

When most new corporations are started, each of the original shareholders generally invests a nominal amount to get the corporation going and look to bank financing or future potential profits for growth and capitalization. The shareholders may simply agree that each will be responsible for his or her pro rata share of future financing requirements through the purchase of more shares if other methods of financing are not readily available or practical.

Problems may arise when one of the shareholders is unwilling to purchase the pro rata share of the future offering; the remedies available to the remaining shareholders can be sought mainly through a shareholders' agreement. This type of situation deals with the *obligation* of a shareholder to participate in future offerings; it is equally important to protect a shareholder's *right* to participate.

Consider a situation where a corporation has two shareholders, one having a majority of shares and the other a minority interest. The majority shareholder may issue a large number of shares to himself or herself, thereby diluting the equity base and decreasing the minority shareholder's overall interest in the corporation. Accordingly, shareholders' agreements generally contain a pro rata right to participate in future offerings of securities and require that no more securities may be offered without the prior approval of, say, two-thirds or three-quarters of the holders of the common shares.

c. RESTRICTIONS ON THE TRANSFER OF SHARES

Unlike public corporations where there can be a wide variety of shareholders, the shareholders of private companies are often few in number and wish to restrict the admission of any new partners into their organization. As a result, however, the marketability of the shares may be affected.

These conflicting considerations, namely the restriction on admission of new partners and the marketability of shares, are often resolved by the use of a "right of first refusal" clause in a shareholders' agreement.

A shareholder wishing to sell shares with this technique must first offer to sell the shares to the other shareholders. If the remaining shareholders do not accept the offer, the offeror is entitled to sell the shares to a third party at a price and on terms not more favorable than those contained in the offer to the remaining shareholders. If the selling shareholder cannot find a buyer and is required to amend the original offer, the procedure must be repeated.

d. BUY-SELL PROVISIONS

Shareholders' agreements may contemplate the purchase by a shareholder of the shares of another shareholder upon the happening of a certain event. This event is most commonly restricted to the death of the shareholder.

The death of a shareholder in a private corporation carries serious implications for both the deceased's estate and the remaining shareholders. As already mentioned, the shares of a private corporation generally have a limited market value so that the personal representative of the deceased's estate may have some difficulty in disposing of them.

The surviving shareholders suddenly have a new partner whom they did not choose; namely, the deceased's personal representative. If the personal representative decides not to sell the deceased's shares to the remaining shareholders, these shareholders may encounter difficulties in managing the corporation should the personal representative take an active part in the day-to-day management of the corporation.

Therefore, many shareholders' agreements contain buy-sell provisions in which the estate of the deceased shareholder would sell, and the surviving shareholders would purchase, all of the shares of the deceased at a specified price or at a price to be determined under the agreement. The buy-sell provisions should cover the following points:

(a) How the purchase is to be funded

(b) How the shares are to be valued to establish a purchase price

Funding the purchase of shares is not a problem for those shareholders with sufficient personal wealth to either pay the purchase price or to persuade a banker to lend them the money. However, it is more common to accomplish funding through business life insurance policies on the lives of all the shareholders.

The corporation may be the beneficiary to which the insurance proceeds go, or the surviving shareholders may receive the proceeds directly. Tax consequences vary with the manner in which the insurance policy is implemented, so you should consult your insurance representative, accountant, and lawyer before proceeding with an insurance funding program.

The valuation of shares to establish a purchase price is often difficult, and no simple solution exists. However, the following techniques are often used:

(a) A fixed amount in the agreement

(b) A formula approach, usually book value, adjusted book value, multiple of earnings, or a combination of assets and earnings

(c) Appraisal by an independent third party such as the corporation's auditors or a business valuator

(d) Annual agreement among the shareholders

(e) A combination of any or all of the above

e. KEEP IT SIMPLE

Shareholders, usually with the best intentions in mind, often instruct their lawyers to draft shareholders' agreements. Once the agreement is executed it is stored with the corporate files and forgotten for years. When a situation arises requiring guidance from the agreement, such as the provisions relating to the purchase of shares, the shareholders are often dismayed to realize that the agreement is far too complicated and cumbersome to carry out its intent, and because of the passage of time, its provisions are out of date.

Therefore, while I recommend that you seek professional advice from your accountant and lawyer before engaging in the negotiation and execution of a shareholders' agreement, make sure that you keep it simple!

The form of shareholders' agreement shown as Sample 27 is a very simple one. It is enclosed for your information only, and legal advice should be sought for further assistance.

AGREEMENT made this 25th day of October, 200–.

BETWEEN:

JOHN DOE, of the Town of Anytown, in the Province of Ontario

(hereinafter "DOE")

OF THE FIRST PART

—and—

JACK GREEN, of the town of Anytown, in the Province of Ontario

(hereinafter "GREEN")

OF THE SECOND PART

—and—

JOHN DOE & ASSOCIATES LTD., a corporation pursuant to the laws of the Province of Ontario

(hereinafter the "Corporation")

OF THE THIRD PART

WHEREAS the authorized capital of the Corporation is to be divided into an unlimited number of common shares;

AND WHEREAS Doe beneficially owns 501 shares and Green beneficially owns 499 common shares, being all the common shares issued and outstanding;

AND WHEREAS Doe and Green (hereinafter collectively referred to as the "SHAREHOLDERS") desire to provide for the constitution, organization, management and supervision of the Corporation, and for the disposition and succession of the common shares thereof;

NOW THEREFORE, in consideration of the mutual covenants and agreements herein contained and subject to the terms and conditions hereinafter set out, the parties hereto agree as follows:

1.00 **CONSTITUTION**

1.01   The Corporation shall not:

   a)   Amend its Article of Incorporation;
   b)   Make an arrangement;
   c)   Amalgamate;
   d)   Apply to a jurisdiction other than the Dominion of Canada for an instrument of
continuation;

pursuant to the Ontario Business Corporations Act, except upon the unanimous consent of the Shareholder.

1.02   The Corporation shall not pass, amend, or rescind any by-law of the Corporation, except upon the unanimous consent of the Shareholders.

1.03   The Corporation shall not:

   a)   Redeem; or
   b)   Purchase for cancellation any of the Shares of the Corporation;

not shall it sanction or approve any:

   c)   Conversion;
   d)   Surrender;
   e)   Allotment;
   f)   Transfer

of the shares of the Corporation, except upon the unanimous consent of the Shareholders, or as hereinafter provided.

2.00   **DIRECTORS**

2.01   The Board of Directors shall manage or supervise the management of the affairs and business of the Corporation.

2.02   The Board of Directors of the Corporation shall consist of a minimum of one and a maximum of three directors. The initial Board of Directors shall consist of three directors and shall include one nominee of Doe and one nominee of Green. The third director shall be elected by the unanimous vote of the shareholders. The number of directors within the minimum and maximun range may be increased or decreased only upon the unanimous consent of the shareholders. If the Board is increased to four directors, then the Board shall consist of two nominees of Doe and two nominees of Green. If the Board of Directors is increased to five directors the Board shall consist of two nominees of Doe and two nominees of Green, and the fifth director shall be elected by the unanimous consent of the shareholders.

2.03   A quorum for the transaction of business at meetings of the Board of Directors shall consist of a majority of directors.

2.04   Except as otherwise provided in this Agreement, all questions proposed for consideration of the Board of Directors at any Board meeting shall, in the presence of a quorum, be determined by a majority of the directors in attendance; provided however, that the affirmative vote of at least one nominee director of Doe and one nominee director of Green shall be required to decide any action of the Board of Directors.

3.00 **ISSUE OF SHARES**

3.01 **Pro Rata Offering**

a) Except as the parties shall otherwise unanimously agree in writing, no shares shall be issued by the Corporation unless, and each offering by the Corporations of shares shall be made, in accordance with paragraph 3.01.

b) Each offer shall be made to the shareholder as nearly as may be in proportion to the number of shares respectively held by them at the date of the offer.

c) Every offer shall be made in writing and shall state that a party which desires to subscribe for shares in excess of its proportion shall, in its subscription specify the number or amount, as the case may be, of shares in excess of its proportion that it desires to purchase. If a shareholder does not subscribe for its proportion, the unsubscribed shares shall be used to satisfy the subscription of the other shareholder for the shares in excess of its proportion. No shareholder shall be bound to take any shares in excess of the amount it so desires.

3.02 **Unsubscribed shares** If all of the shares of any issue are not subscribe for within a period of 45 days after the same are offered to the parties pursuant to the provisions of paragraph 3.01, the Corporation may, during the next three months, offer and sell all or any of the shares not taken up by the parties but the price at which shares may be allotted and sold shall not be less than the subscription price offered to the parties pursuant to paragraph 3.01 and on terms more favorable than those offered to the parties.

3.03 **Additional Parties** Every issue of shares shall be subject to the condition that the subscriber thereof shall, if not a party hereto, agree to be bound by the terms of this agreement.

4.00 **DISPOSITION OF SHARES**

4.01 **Purchase Rights** If any shareholder (the "Offeror") desires or is required by law to transfer any of his shares to another person, or to sell or dispose of any share, the other shareholder (the "Offeree") shall have the prior right to purchase the shares on the terms and in accordance with the procedure contained in paragraph 4.02.

4.02 **Procedure on Transfers**

a) An Offeror shall notify the Corporation in writing of his desire or intention to transfer, sell or otherwise dispose of any share. The notice (the "Selling Notice") shall set out:

(i) the number and a brief description of each class of shares;
(ii) the price and terms of payment which the Offeror is willing to accept for the shares;
and
(iii) if the Offeror has received an offer to purchase the shares, the name and address of the potential purchaser and the terms of payment and price contained in this offer.

b) The shares shall then be offered to the Offeree on the terms of payment and for the price contained in the Selling Notice, and shall remain open for acceptance ad hereinafter provided for a period of 45 days.

c) If, within that period the Offeree does not agree to purchase all of the shares offered, he shall be deemed to have refused to purchase the shares offered, and the Offeror may offer and sell all of the shares offered to any other person at the price and on the terms and conditions set out in the Selling Notice.

d) If all of the shares offered shall be accepted by the Offeree, the shares shall be sold to him for the price and on the terms contained in the Selling Notice.

4.03 **Additional Parties** Every transfer of shares shall be subject to the condition that the purchaser thereof shall, if not a party hereto, agree to be bound by the terms of this agreement.

4.04   **Release from Liability** If a sale, transfer or other disposition of shares is completed in accordance with this Article, the Offeror shall upon completion of the purchase be indemnified by the other shareholders from all liability or in respect of the Corporation whether under the provisions of this agreement or under any guarantee, indemnity or other financial assistance given in respect of the operations in the Corporation arising after the date of sale, transfer or other disposition and the purchase of the shares offered shall assume all obligations in respect thereof.

5.00   **GENERAL**

5.01   a)   This Agreement may be terminated upon:

(i)   written notice from one of the shareholders to the other;
(ii)   the bankruptcy or insolvency of either party;
(iii)   the enactment of any legislation requiring the dissolution of the Corporation or rendering its continued operation illegal.

b)   The Corporation shall thereupon be dissolved unless where termination occurs pursuant to paragraph 5.01 (a)(i), one of the shareholders agrees to purchase the shares of the other upon terms and conditions that they mutually agree.

5.02   **Assignment** The agreement is not assignable by any party except insofar as its benefit and burden pass with equity securities transferred in accordance with the agreement. This agreement shall enure to the benefit of and be binding upon the heirs, executors, administrators, successors, or any other legal representatives of the parties hereto.

5.03   **Additional Parties** Every issue and transfer of shares shall be subject to the condition that each subscriber or transferee, as the case may be, shall. if not a party hereto, agree to be bound by the terms hereof and become a party hereto by executing an agreement to be bound hereby.

5.04   **Miscellaneous**

a)   The Shareholders shall not sell, assign, transfer, mortgage, charge, pledge or hypothecate their shares except pursuant to the terms hereof or except upon the unanimous consent of the shareholders.

b)   In the event of any conflict between the terms of this agreement and the Articles of Incorporation and By-laws of the Corporation, the terms of this agreement shall prevail and the parties hereto shall forthwith cause such necessary alterations to be made to the Articles of Incorporation and By-laws as are required so as to resolve the conflict.

5.05   **Third Party Payments** Any arrangements made by the parties hereto with third parties and all payments to the third parties are the responsibility of the party entering into such arrangement and not of the other party.

IN WITNESS WHEREOF the parties hereto have executed this Agreement as of the date first above mentioned.

SIGNED, SEALED and DELIVERED
in the presence of

_____
JOHN DOE

_____
JACK GREEN

JOHN DOE & ASSOCIATES LTD.

Per: _____

9
RUNNING YOUR CORPORATION SMOOTHLY

a. ANNUAL GENERAL MEETING

All corporations are required to hold an annual general meeting of shareholders no later than 18 months after the date of incorporation. All subsequent general meetings must be held 15 months after the preceding meeting. The annual meetings are held at such place in or outside Ontario as the directors determine, or at the registered office of the corporation, subject to any other designation in the Articles or a unanimous shareholders' agreement. For example, if the Articles or a unanimous shareholders' agreement provide for holding a meeting at a place outside Ontario, the meetings can be held at that particular place.

The Business Corporations Act (Ontario) provides that at least 10 days' and not more than 50 days' notice of the meeting is required in the case of shareholders in a private corporation. In most cases, formal notice provisions are not required, as the shareholders are notified orally and may waive the notice informally by appearing at the meeting or formally by entering the waiver in the minutes of the meeting.

1. Common items dealt with at a meeting

For a small private corporation, the Business Corporations Act (Ontario) provides that a financial statement for the period from incorporation or from the last annual general meeting to a date not more than six months before the present meeting is to be laid before the shareholders at the meeting.

The financial statements must include at least a balance sheet, a statement of retained earnings, an income statement, and a statement of changes in financial position. If the corporation has appointed an auditor, an auditor's report must also be given. By-laws and resolutions passed by the directors in the previous year are ratified.

Other business that is usually conducted is the appointment of directors and, if the shareholders do not waive it, the appointment of auditors.

2. Why hold a meeting?

The annual general meeting also provides a useful opportunity to go over the business and allow those shareholders who perhaps do not take an active part in the business to make their contribution (or complaints).

If you decide not to formally hold an annual general meeting, you may have all the shareholders consent in writing to all the resolutions that could or would normally be passed at a formal meeting (see Sample 28). Many small corporations find this a more convenient way to go about the business of holding an annual general meeting.

b. ALL ABOUT SHAREHOLDERS AND DIRECTORS

The following summary of the rights and responsibilities imposed on directors and shareholders is for your information only. If the relationships in a small, closely held corporation deteriorate to such an extent that these rights are exercised, the corporation would probably cease being effective. However, by reading this section over carefully, you will gain a better idea of what is expected of shareholders and directors.

In lieu of the 200– Annual General Meeting of the Corporation, the following resolutions are consented to in writing by all the shareholders of the Corporation entitled to attend and vote at an Annual General Meeting of the Corporation, as evidenced by their signatures hereto.

ELECTION OF DIRECTORS

Resolved: John Albert Doe be elected director of the Corporation until the next Annual General Meeting of the Corporation.

APPROVAL OF ACTS OF DIRECTORS AND OFFICERS OF THE CORPORATION

Resolved: That all of the acts, contracts, by-laws, resolutions, proceedings, and payments made, done, and taken by the Directors and Officers of the Corporation since incorporation of the Corporation be and the same are hereby approved, ratified, and confirmed.

FINANCIAL STATEMENTS

Resolved: That the financial statements of the Corporation to January 31, 200– are hereby approved.

WAIVER OF APPOINTMENT OF AUDITOR

The undersigned, being all the shareholders of the Corporation, hereby consent that the Corporation shall be exempt from the provisions of Part XII of the Ontario Business Corporations Act regarding the appointment and duties of an auditor in respect of the financial year of the Corporation ending January 31, 200-.

Resolved: That the Corporation hereby waives the appointment of an auditor for the corporation for the present financial year, pursuant to Part XII of the Ontario Business Corporations Act.

Resolved: That Mr. Charles Brown, CA be and he is hereby appointed accountant of the Corporation to hold office until the next annual meeting or until a successor is appointed at a remuneration to be fixed by the directors, the directors being authorized to fix such remuneration, and the Secretary is hereby directed to give the Corporation's accountant written notice of his appointment.

The foregoing resolutions are hereby passed by all the Shareholders of the Corporation as of the 14th day of June, 200–.

JAD

John A. Doe

Being all the shareholders of the Corporation entitled to vote at meetings of shareholders.

1. Your rights as a shareholder

At one time all shareholders' rights were contained in the body of cases that formed the common law. Now the trend is to codify these rights in the act that governs corporations in each province. The following sections discuss the major parts of the Ontario Business Corporations Act.

(a) Oppressive and prejudicial conduct

The book *Palmer on Company Law* says:

> It has always been the law that if a majority acts in oppression of the minority, the latter may petition the court to wind up the corporation, on the grounds that it is just and equitable to do so.

This remedy is for wrongs done to a shareholder, creditor, director, or officer and not wrongs done to the corporation. To wind up the corporation under section 207 of the Ontario Business Corporations Act, you must show that there are grounds because the affairs of the corporation are conducted in an oppressive manner. What conduct is oppressive depends on the facts of each case. You, the applicant, will have to tell the court the type of conduct you are complaining about (e.g., "share dilution" or the sale of the major business and assets of the corporation without proper shareholder approval).

The court will exercise its discretion in determining if the application for the winding-up order is made for honest reasons, and if such a step would be in the best interests of the corporation.

Frequently this remedy is not effective because the real assets of the corporation consist of the skill, knowledge, and business acumen of the directors and/or shareholders, not physical assets with a high retail value. So this type of remedy may not be a remedy at all for the oppressed shareholder since the benefit of these intangible items is lost when the corporation is broken up and its assets sold.

Furthermore, courts have been reluctant to order a winding up of a corporation, so that aggrieved shareholders have been left with little recourse to enforce their personal rights. Therefore, a shareholder may apply to the court for an order the court thinks fit in the circumstances, including the following:

(a) An order restraining the conduct complained of

(b) An order appointing a receiver

(c) An order directing an issue or exchange of shares

(d) An order appointing new directors

(e) An order directing the corporation to purchase the shares of a particular shareholder

(f) An order compensating the aggrieved person

(g) An order winding up the corporation

(b) Derivative actions on behalf of the corporation

As in the previous section, the concern here is with the right of a shareholder, who is generally a minority (i.e., those controlling less than 50 percent of the voting shares), to bring an action on behalf of the corporation or any of its subsidiaries when the corporation is being damaged and the directors and officers have not started legal proceedings to protect it.

Because it is really the corporation that is suffering the harm, theoretically the corporation, via the directors, should be the entity that brings the action. However, the minority in this case cannot get the board of directors to take the necessary steps, so the minority shareholders are forced to sue as representatives of the corporation.

To permit an action to be started, the court must be satisfied that —

(a) the directors of the corporation or its subsidiary will not bring, diligently prosecute, or defend or discontinue the action;

(b) the person applying to the court is acting in good faith;

(c) it appears to be in the best interest of the corporation or its subsidiary that the action be brought; and

(d) the person applying to the court has given 14 days' notice to the directors of his or her intention to apply to the court.

After hearing the application, the court may make any order it thinks fit, including for example —

(a) an order authorizing the person applying, or any other person, to control the conduct of the action;

(b) an order giving directions for the conduct of the action;

(c) an order directing that any amount payable from a defendant in the action be paid directly to the shareholders and former shareholders; and

(d) an order requiring the corporation to pay the shareholder's legal fees incurred in connection with the action.

(c) Rights of dissenting shareholders

The right to dissent can be exercised by the members of a small, closely held private corporation when the directors and/or majority shareholders propose major changes that materially affect the nature of minority shareholders' investment. Basically, this provision allows a shareholder to demand that the corporation purchase his or her shares at fair market value under certain conditions of dissent. All of the following events entitle a shareholder of a private corporation to dissent under this provision:

(a) When a shareholder has dissented on a corporate resolution approving certain amendments to the Articles, amalgamations, sale of all or substantially all of its property.

(b) If there has been a compulsory acquisition of shares after the acquirer has received 90 percent of the shares via takeover bid, holders of the remaining 10 percent of the shares may be forced to sell their shares and demand "fair value" from the acquirer.

(c) If 90 percent of the shares of the corporation are acquired by one person, holders of the remaining 10 percent may demand "fair value" for their shares from the corporation.

(d) When there is a termination of shareholders in a "going private" transaction.

The procedures for a shareholder to dissent and invoke this appraisal right vary depending on whether the right is triggered by a fundamental change under situation (a) above or under a compulsory acquisition under (b) and (c).

Complex rules provide for a voluntary settlement of fair value followed by procedures for seeking the court's assistance.

This right may not be much help, however, if the corporation is insolvent, as all corporations are prohibited from purchasing shares if the purchase or redemption of their own shares would make them bankrupt or unable to meet their debts as they become due.

(d) The right to requisition a meeting

The holders of not less than 5 percent of the issued shares that carry the right to vote at a shareholders' meeting may requisition the directors to call a meeting. The purpose of the meeting must be stated in the requisition.

The corporation must reimburse the person who submitted the requisition for expenses as long as he or she acted in good faith in the interests of the shareholders.

The court may requisition a shareholders' meeting if a shareholder or director applies to the court. The meeting must be conducted in the manner the court directs.

2. Shareholders' liabilities

One of the advantages of being incorporated is "limited liability," but there are times when this limited liability is not applicable. When the stated capital of the corporation is reduced, each person who was a shareholder on the date of the reduction is individually liable to the corporation's creditors for the amount of money paid to them as a result of the reduction.

To the extent that a unanimous shareholders' agreement restricts the powers of the directors to supervise the management of the business, the directors are relieved of that liability and each shareholder assumes that liability.

If the corporation is dissolved and its property distributed to the shareholders, each shareholder is liable to a claimant of the corporation to the extent of the amount received by the shareholder.

Furthermore, it is common for banks and other lending institutions to obtain a personal guarantee from the directors or shareholders of the corporation before they will lend money to the corporation. If you personally guarantee a loan to your corporation, you are liable as guarantor for the repayment of the loan to the lender.

3. Directors' rights and duties

All private, closely held corporations require a minimum of one director. (Public, distributing corporations require a minimum of three.)

The number of directors can be fixed in the Articles of Incorporation or can be a minimum and maximum. The corporation may amend its Articles to increase or decrease the fixed number or the minimum and maximum.

When the Articles provide for a minimum and maximum number of directors, the number of directors to be elected is decided from time to time by a special resolution. The corporation must file a certified copy of the special resolution with the Companies Branch within 15 days after it is passed.

A properly completed Notice of Change must also be filed. A majority of the directors must be resident Canadians. All directors must be of sound mind, 18 years of age or older, and not bankrupt.

In order to conduct business at a meeting of directors, a majority of those present at the meeting must be resident Canadians. A director can be considered present at a meeting if he or she communicates with the other directors by telephone.

Of course, you may avoid having meetings by having resolutions drawn up and circulated to all of the directors for their signatures.

Directors are responsible for conducting the business affairs of the corporation. Directors, and the officers they hire, are required to act honestly and to exercise the skill and care of a reasonably prudent person in carrying out their duties. The following is a brief summary of some of the other duties imposed upon directors by the Business Corporations Act (Ontario).

(a) Duty of disclosure

Basically the object of this provision is to prevent directors from making a personal profit to the detriment of the corporation. A director who has a material personal interest in a contract that is important to the corporation is obliged to disclose the nature and extent of his or her interest in the contract to the other directors at the first meeting in which the contract is discussed. After the nature and extent of the director's interest is disclosed, he or she is required to abstain from voting and is not to be considered in the quorum of directors.

If the director's interest in the transaction arises after the transaction is first discussed, he or she must inform the other directors at the next meeting.

If a director fails to make a disclosure in the fashion described, he or she may have the contract ratified by the shareholders by special resolution, if the director acted honestly and in good faith, the transaction was fair and reasonable, and disclosure is made to the shareholders.

A director would be wise to do this because the shareholder approval would allow him or her to keep any personal profit that might otherwise have to be returned to the corporation.

Where a director has not disclosed an interest in a contract, the corporation or a shareholder may apply to the court for an order setting aside the contract or transaction, and directing that the director account to the corporation for any profit or gain realized.

(b) The duty to keep informed

Directors are liable to creditors and, in certain circumstances, to the corporation if they authorize —

(a) financial assistance to a shareholder, director, officer, or employee;

(b) the purchase, redemption, or acquisition of its shares;

(c) the payment of a commission; or

(d) the payment of a dividend,

and by reason of these expenditures the corporation is unable to meet its debts as they become due.

Every director and officer must act honestly and in good faith in the best interests of the corporation and exercise the care and diligence of a reasonably prudent person in comparable circumstances.

A director may avoid liability for a resolution if his or her dissent is recorded in the minutes of the meeting in which the resolution was passed. If he or she was not present at the meeting in which the resolution giving rise to the liability was passed, then the director can file a dissent within seven days of becoming aware of the resolution. He or she can also send this dissent to the corporation by registered mail.

This liability is one of the major reasons why directors who are not actively involved in the day-to-day operation of the corporation should carefully read a financial statement and keep in touch with the corporation's accountant. The problem of ignorance of the true state of corporate affairs is less likely to arise in well-run small corporations than it is in large, loosely organized corporations.

All incumbent directors are entitled to see financial statements and corporate records at any reasonable time. Retired directors can look at financial records for the period in which they held office.

(c) Liability for wages

Directors are jointly and severally liable for the unpaid wages of employees of the corporation. The maximum amount the directors are liable for is six months' wages and vacation pay accruing for up to twelve months. A director must be sued for the debt within six months after collection proceedings against the corporation proved ineffective. The suit must be brought against the director while he or she is acting as a director or within six months of his or her retirement. The Ontario Ministry of Labour is very efficient at helping employees quickly process wage claims, so this liability is not something to be treated lightly.

All directors of newly formed corporations should keep this responsibility in mind before they sign up as an incorporator or before consenting to act as a director. (Incorporators and those who sign consent forms are directors until the shareholders officially appoint directors for the corporation.)

4. Directors' indemnification

Directors are entitled to benefit from liability insurance taken out on their behalf by the corporation. This money may be used to indemnify directors and officers from liability for costs, charges, and expenses sustained in a lawsuit against the director, or against the corporation, for acts done or permitted by him or her in the execution of the duties of the office.

However, the purchase of insurance policies is not a foolproof way of protecting yourself as a director. No corporation is entitled to indemnify a director whom a court has found to be dishonest or in breach of a duty.

A further consideration is that for most small, new corporations, the premiums on insurance policies for the directors may be prohibitively high.

5. Appointment and removal of directors

All directors may be appointed by either signing the Articles of Incorporation as first directors or by being elected by the shareholders in a general meeting in accordance with the by-laws of the corporation. The people named as first directors in the Articles of Incorporation act as directors until others are elected by the shareholders. Directors may hold office for a term expiring not later than the third annual meeting of shareholders after they were elected. The length of term may be specified in the by-laws. At the end of the term of office, the director may be re-elected.

The shareholders may vote a director out of office at any time by calling a special meeting for the removal of the director and passing an ordinary resolution for the removal of the director.

If there has been a change in the people who are directors, either at a specially called meeting or at the annual general meeting, a Notice of Change must be filed indicating the names and addresses of the people who are now directors and the names and addresses of those who left the position.

Officers of the corporation may be dismissed at any time by an ordinary resolution of the directors at a directors' meeting. A dismissal by the directors, however, does not prevent an officer from relying on a contract of employment with the corporation and either being paid a sum in settlement for wrongful dismissal, if such is the case, or suing the corporation for breach of contract.

10

HOW TO CHANGE YOUR CORPORATE NAME

After you have been operating for a number of years you may come to the conclusion that the name "Slipshod Industries Ltd." is not really for you. Perhaps your name no longer reflects what you do. For example, you may no longer produce silver jewellery exclusively, and customers may be deterred, by reason of the increased interest in gold jewellery, from looking at products supplied by Sam the Silversmith Ltd. Or, you may have incorporated with your own name and now regret it as you get midnight telephone calls from stranded motorists who are able to trace your personal phone from a name like Marvin Mechanic's Towing Services Ltd. Finally, you may feel a little uncomfortable with a name like North End Appliance Repairs now that you do business and operate out of the south end of town.

These are only a few of the many reasons there are for changing your corporate name. Whatever your reason is, it is simple to change your name in Ontario by amending your Articles under section 168 of the Ontario Business Corporations Act. Of course, the name clearance procedure for the new name must be completed before your Articles may be amended (see chapter 3). However, once this is done, you may purchase the Articles of Amendment (Form 3) from your local stationer and fill it out in a manner similar to Sample 29. The Articles of Amendment are simple to complete for the purposes of changing your corporate name.

First, you have to pass a special resolution authorizing the change of name. This resolution should be recorded in the minutes of a special meeting or by the passage of a special resolution in writing. The manner in which the articles of the corporation are amended is set out in paragraph 4 of the Articles of Amendment, which are filed in duplicate.

A fee of $150 payable to the Minister of Finance and a NUANS name search report relating to your new corporation must accompany your Articles of Amendment. If you pay by cheque, write the name of your corporation on the face of the cheque. You do not avoid legal liabilities by changing your corporate name. All debts and obligations incurred by the corporation in its old name remain the responsibility of the corporation under the new name.

The definition of a special resolution from the Business Corporations Act (Ontario) is reproduced for your convenience below:

1(1) "special resolution" means a resolution that is

(a) submitted to a special meeting of the shareholders of a corporation duly called for the purpose of considering the resolution and passed, with or without amendment, at the meeting by at least two-thirds of the votes cast, or

(b) consented to in writing by each shareholder of the corporation entitled to vote at such a meeting or the shareholder's attorney authorized in writing;

The special resolution should be filed in the minute book. In most small, closely held corporations a special resolution is usually passed by having all of the shareholders sign it or consent in writing to the resolution changing the name.

If a corporation has a number name, the authority for changing its name can rest with the directors. In other words, the directors may approve the name change at a special meeting of the Board or by written resolution.

SAMPLE 29
ARTICLES OF AMENDMENT

Ontario Corporation Number
Numéro de la société en Ontario

1

444444

ARTICLES OF AMENDMENT
STATUTS DE MODIFICATION

1. The name of the corporation is: (Set out in BLOCK CAPITAL LETTERS)
    Dénomination sociale actuelle de la société (écrire en LETTRES MAJUSCULES SEULEMENT) :

| J | O | H | N | | D | O | E | | & | | A | S | S | O | C | I | A | T | E | S | | L | I | M | I | T | E | D | |

2. The name of the corporation is changed to (if applicable): (Set out in BLOCK CAPITAL LETTERS)
    Nouvelle dénomination sociale de la société (s'il y a lieu) (écrire en LETTRES MAJUSCULES SEULMENT) :

| P | E | R | S | O | N | A | B | L | E | | P | E | R | S | O | N | N | E | L | | L | T | D | . | | | | |

3. Date of incorporation/amalgamation:
    Date de la constitution ou de la fusion :

    200-, JANUARY, 15

    (Year, Month, Day)
    (année, mois, jour)

4. Complete only if there is a change in the number of directors or the minimum / maximum numbers of directors.
    Il faut remplir cette partie seulement si le nombre d'administrateurs ou si le nombre minimal ou maximal d' administrateurs a changé.

    Number of directors is/are: or   minimum and maximum number of directors is/are:
    Nombre d'administrateurs :   ou   *nombres minimum et maximum d'administrateurs :*

    Number   or   minimum and maximum
    Nombre   ou   *minimum et maximum*

5. The articles of the corporation are amended as follows:
    Les status de la société sont modifiés de la façon suivante :

    TO CHANGE THE NAME OF THE CORPORATION TO PERSONABLE PERSONNEL LTD.

106

2

6. The amendment has been duly authorized as required by sections 168 and 170 (as applicable) of the *Business Corporations Act*.
   La modification a été dûment autorisée conformément aux articles 168 et 170 (selon le cas) de la Loi sur les Sociétes par actions.

7. The resolution authorizing the amendment was approved by the shareholders/directors (as applicable) of the corporation on
   Les actionnaires ou les administrateurs (selon le cas) de la société ont approuvé la résolution autorisant la modification le

200-, AUGUST, 29

(Year, Month, Day)
(année, mois, jour)

These articles are signed in duplicate.
Les présents statuts sont signés en double exemplaire.

JOHN DOE & ASSOCIATES LIMITED

(Name of Corporation) (If the name is to be changed by these articles, set out current name)
(Dénomination sociale de la société) (Si l'on demande un changement de nom, indiquer ci-dessus la dénomination sociale actuelle)

By/
Par :

_____
JAD
Signature
(Signature)

PRESIDENT
_____
(Description of Office)
(Fonction)

JOHN ALBERT DOE

11
HOW TO DISSOLVE YOUR CORPORATION

If you decide that you no longer want to carry on business as a corporation, you may apply to the Companies Branch to dissolve it. For example, your corporation may have been inactive for several years and you wish to rid yourself of the annual paperwork required in filing corporate tax returns. Or, you and the other owners may wish to retire and you are unable to find someone to take over the business.

To dissolve a corporation, the shareholders must either —

(a) *all* agree to the dissolution in writing (see Sample 30), or

(b) pass a special resolution in favor of dissolution at a shareholders' meeting.

The written consent must be obtained from all the shareholders who would have been entitled to vote at a meeting.

Alternatively, a corporation may be dissolved upon the authorization of all its incorporators at any time within two years of its date of incorporation if the corporation has not commenced business and has not issued any shares.

Before the Articles of Dissolution can be filed, several other matters must be taken care of.

You must also obtain a Certificate of Consent from the Corporations Tax Branch of the Ministry of Finance in Oshawa. This must accompany your Articles of Dissolution when they are sent for filing. The Certificate of Consent is valid for 60 days from the date of issuance, so you should make sure you file your Articles of Dissolution within that period.

You should also get a Clearance Certificate from Canada Customs and Revenue Agency indicating that all federal corporate taxes are paid. This certificate is not essential for filing Articles of Dissolution, but it is advisable to get one anyway. Contact your local Canada Customs and Revenue Agency office.

Before dissolving your corporation, you must also pay all debts owing or have your creditors consent to the dissolution (see Sample 31). Any debts payable to unknown creditors may be paid to the Public Guardian and Trustee for the Province of Ontario.

All notices and returns required under the Corporations Information Act (Ontario) must also be filed with the Companies and Personal Property Security Branch (CPPSB) prior to dissolution.

Now the assets of the corporation can be distributed rateably to all of the shareholders. "Rateable distribution" means a distribution according to the interests of the shareholders in the corporation (i.e., related to the number of shares, promissory notes, and dividends owing to them). All the shareholders can enter into an agreement concerning the disposal of any remaining assets.

Once all these requirements are met, you file the Articles of Dissolution in duplicate (see Sample 32). For a corporation that has started business and issued shares, or has been in existence for more than two years, the Articles must be signed by an officer or director, and the signatures must be originals, not photocopies.

As earlier noted, Articles of Dissolution must be accompanied by a written consent to the dissolution from the Corporations Tax Branch, Ministry of Finance. The filing fee for Articles of Dissoluton is $25, payable to the Minister of Finance.

File these papers with the CPPSB of the Ministry of Consumer and Business Services. Once the Certificate of Dissolution is issued by the Minister, your corporation no longer exists. You should advise all tax department, city assessment, and licensing offices that your corporation is now dissolved, and that your corporation's last filing with them is final. You should also cancel your GST registration number. This helps tie up loose ends. After dissolution, you should retain the corporate records of the corporation for six years, after which time they can be destroyed.

It is important to note that despite the dissolution of a corporation, any shareholder who receives any property is liable to any person claiming under section 242 of the Business Corporations Act (Ontario) to the extent of the amount received by the shareholder upon the distribution of its assets. An action to enforce any liability may be brought within five years after the date of dissolution.

In essence, section 242 of the Business Corporations Act (Ontario) provides that despite the dissolution of a corporation, an action or proceeding commenced by or against a corporation before its dissolution may be continued as if the corporation had not been dissolved, and an action may be brought against a corporation as if it had not been dissolved.

In that event, property that would have been available to satisfy a judgment remains available for that purpose. That would include any land that belonged to a corporation immediately before its dissolution. Such land would remain available to be sold in power of sale proceedings.

SAMPLE 30
RESOLUTION FOR DISSOLUTION

Special Resolution of the Shareholders of
John Doe & Associates Ltd.
(the "Corporation")

BE IT RESOLVED THAT:

1. The Corporation be dissolved pursuant to section 237 of the Ontario Business Corporations Act.

2. As incidental to the foregoing, the property of the Corporation be distributed rateably among the shareholders of the Corporation according to their rights and interests in the Corporation.

3. The directors and officers are hereby authorized and directed to do, sign, and execute all things, deeds, and documents necessary or desirable for the due carrying out of the foregoing.

The foregoing special resolution is hereby consented to by all the shareholders of the Corporation pursuant to the Business Corporations Act (Ontario).

DATED the 20th day of October, 200–.

JAD

John A. Doe

SAMPLE 31
CONSENT OF CREDITORS TO DISSOLUTION

CONSENT OF CREDITORS TO DISSOLUTION

TO: JOHN DOE & ASSOCIATES LIMITED

The undersigned being a creditor of the Corporation hereby consents to its dissolution pursuant to section 237 of the Business Corporations Act (Ontario).

DATED the 20th day of October, 200–

C. Creditor
Cameron Creditor

SAMPLE 32
ARTICLES OF DISSOLUTION

For Ministry Use Only
À l'usage exclusif du ministère

Ontario Corporation Number
Numéro de la société en Ontario

ARTICLES OF DISSOLUTION
STATUTS DE DISSOLUTION

Form 10
Business
Corporations
Act

*Formule 10
Loi sur les
sociétés par
actions*

1. The name of the corporation is: (Set out in BLOCK CAPITAL LETTERS)
Dénomination sociale de la société : (Écrire en LETTRES MAJUSCULES SEULEMENT)

J	O	H	N		D	O	E		&		A	S	S	O	C	I	A	T	E	S		L	T	D	.				

2. Date of incorporation/amalgamation:
Date de la constitution ou de la fusion :

   200-, January, 07

   (Year, Month,Day)
   (année, mois, jour)

3. The dissolution has been duly authorized under clause 237 (a) or (b) (as applicable) of the *Business Corporations Act.*
   La dissolution de la société a été dûment approuvée aux termes de l'alinéa 237 a) ou b) (le cas échéant) de la Loi sur les sociétés par actions.

4. The corporation has, (Mark (X) in the box beside the one statement that applies.)
   La société, selon le cas : (cocher la case appropriée)

   [X] (A) no debts, obligations or liabilities;
   (A) n'a ni dettes, ni obligations, ni passif;

   [ ] (B) duly provided for its debts, obligations or liabilities in accordance with subsection 238 (3) of the *Business Corporations Act;*
   (B) a pourvu à ses dettes, à ses obligations ou à son passif conformément au paragraphe 238(3) de la Loi sur les sociétés par actions;

   [ ] (C) obtained consent to its dissolution from its creditors or other persons having interests in its debts, obligations or liabilities.
   (C) a obtenu de ses créanciers ou des autres intéressés à ses dettes, à ses obligations ou à son passif, le consentement à sa dissolution.

5. After satisfying the interests of creditors in all its debts, obligations and liabilities, if any, the corporation has,
   (Mark (X) in the box beside the one statement that applies.)
   Après avoir désintéressé tous ses créanciers, s'il y a lieu, la société, selon le cas :
   (cocher la case appropriée)

   [X] (A) no property to distribute among its shareholders; **or**
   *(A) n'a plus de biens à répartir entre ses actionnaires; **ou***

   [ ] (B) distributed its remaining property rateably among its shareholders according to their rights and interests in the corporation or in accordance with subsection 238 (4) of the *Business Corporations* Act where applicable.
   (B) a réparti les biens qui lui restaient entre ses actionnaires au prorata de leurs droits dans la société ou conformément au paragraphe 238 (4) de la Loi sur les sociétés par actions, s'il y a lieu.

07122 (04/2003)

111

2

6. There are no proceedings pending in any court against the corporation.
   Aucune instance n'est en cours contre la société.

7. The corporation has obtained the consent of the Corporations Tax Branch of the Ministry of Finance to the dissolution and has filed all notices and returns required under the *Corporations Information Act.*
   La Direction de l'imposition des compagnies du ministère des Finances a approuvé la dissolution de la société. La société a déposé tous les avis et rapports requis par la Loi sur les renseignements exigés des personnes morales.

These articles are signed in duplicate.
Les présents statuts sont signés en double exemplaire.

JOHN DOE & ASSOCIATES LTD.
(Name of Corporation)
(Dénomination sociale de la société)

By
Par :

JAD

(Signature)
(Signature)

President
(Description of Office)
(Fonction)

07122 (04/2003)

112

12

REGISTRATION OF OUT-OF-PROVINCE CORPORATIONS

a. CANADIAN CORPORATIONS

If your corporation was incorporated under the laws of a province other than Ontario, or incorporated federally, you may carry on any business in Ontario or hold land in Ontario without obtaining a licence to do so.

The only requirement is to file an Initial Return within 60 days of beginning business activities in Ontario. An extra-provincial or federal corporation must file an Initial Return — Form 2 (see Sample 33).

On the Initial Return — Form 2, you must state the corporation name, the name under which the corporation will do business in Ontario, the name and address of the corporation's manager or chief executive in Ontario (including the date such person was appointed [optional]), and the location of the corporation's registered office in Ontario.

The Initial Return must be signed by a director or officer or a person having knowledge of the affairs of the corporation. The document must be typewritten or printed in block letters.

b. CORPORATIONS INCORPORATED OUTSIDE CANADA

If your corporation has been incorporated or continued outside of Canada, you must apply for an extra-provincial licence to carry on business or hold land in Ontario, or to maintain an action in an Ontario court dealing with a contract made by the corporation.

Under the Extra-Provincial Corporations Act, an extra-provincial corporation carries on business in Ontario if —

(a) it has a resident agent, representative, warehouse office, or place where it carries on its business in Ontario;

(b) it holds an interest, otherwise than by way of securities, in real property situated in Ontario; or

(c) it otherwise carries on business in Ontario.

Furthermore, an extra-provincial corporation does not carry on its business in Ontario if it only takes orders or buys or sells goods, wares, and merchandise; or if it offers or sells services of any type by use of travellers or through advertising or correspondence.

If you are in doubt whether or not your corporation carries on business in Ontario, I suggest that you contact a lawyer or the Companies and Personal Property Security Branch (CPPSB) for help.

The first step toward registration of a corporation incorporated outside of Canada is to satisfy yourself that the name is available. To do this you must obtain from a private search house an Ontario biased or weighted NUANS computer printed search report on the proposed name. The report must be dated not more than 90 days before submission of the application of an extra-provincial licence.

Once you have satisfied yourself that the name is available (which may include obtaining consents of existing registrations), the following documents must be completed and filed with the CPPSB:

(a) An Application for Extra-Provincial Licence in duplicate (see Sample 34)

(b) An Appointment of Agent for Service (see Sample 35)

(c) A Certificate of Status issued under the seal of office and signed by the proper officer (e.g., Director, Corporations Branch) of the jurisdiction to which the corporation is subject and stating the name of the corporation, the date of incorporation, amalgamation or merger, the jurisdiction to which the corporation is subject, and that the corporation is a valid and subsisting corporation

(d) The original cleared NUANS name search report

Both copies of the application for extra-provincial licence must be signed by an officer or director of the corporation, and the name of the corporation must be set out above the signatures. The corporate seal (if one exists) must be affixed to both copies of the application. If the jurisdiction to which the corporation is subject does not require its corporations to have a corporate seal, please indicate so when submitting the application.

When appointing an agent for service of documents, the agent must be a person 18 years of age or older residing in Ontario, or a corporation (other than the applicant) having its registered office in Ontario. Where the agent is a corporation, the consent to act as agent for service must be executed in the name of the corporation under the signature of an officer or director of the corporation which is to act as the agent.

The fee to register an extra-provincial corporation is $330. The application fee for an existing extra-provincial corporation to obtain an amended extra-provincial licence is $150.

All newly licensed corporations must file an Initial Notice — Form 2 as shown in Sample 33.

Notice of any changes in the information contained in the form must be filed within 15 days of the change taking place. In that case, you would file another Form 2 and write an X in the box "notice of change."

SAMPLE 33
INITIAL NOTICE OF EXTRA-PROVINCIAL COMPANY — FORM 2

Ontario

| Ministry of Consumer and Business Services | Ministère des Services aux consommateurs et aux entreprises | Companies and Personal Property Security Branch 393 University Ave, Suite 200 Toronto ON M5G 2M2 | Direction des compagnies et des sûretés mobilières 393, av. University, bureau 200 Toronto ON M5G 2M2 | Page 1/Page 1 |

FORM 2- EXTRA PROVINCIAL CORPORATIONS/
FORMULE 2 - PERSONNES MORALES EXTRA-PROVINCIALES
Please type or print all information in block capital letters using black ink.
Prière de dactylographier les renseignements ou de les écrire en caractères d'imprimerie à l'encre noire.

INITIAL RETURN/NOTICE OF CHANGE /
Corporations Information Act
RAPPORT INITIAL/AVIS DE MODIFICATION
Loi sur les renseignements exigés des personnes morales

| For Ministry Use Only À l'usage du ministère seulement | 2. Ontario Corporation Number Numéro matricule de la personne morale en Ontario | 3. Date of Incorporation or Amalgamation Date de constitution, ou fusion Year/Année Month/Mois Day/Jour 200- 10 16 | 1. Business Corporations/ Société par actions Not-For-Profit Corporation/ Personne morale sans but lucratif | Initial Return Rapport initial [X] | Notice of Change Avis de modification |

4. Corporation Name Including Punctuation/Raison sociale de la personne morale, y compris la ponctuation

I.B. OUTSIDER FABRICATIONS LTD.

For Ministry Use Only
À l'usage du ministère seulement

5. Address of Registered or Head Office/Adresse du siège social

For Ministry Use Only
À l'usage du ministère seulement

c/o / a/s

| Street No./N° civique 321 | Street Name/Nom de la rue BIG CITY | Suite/Bureau 123 |

Street Name (cont'd)/Nom de la rue (suite)

| City/Town/Ville NEW YORK | Province, State/Province, État NEW YORK |
| Country/Pays USA | Postal Code/Code postal 012345 |

6. Address of Principal Office in Ontario/Adresse du bureau principal en Ontario

Street No./N° civique
104

☐ Same as Above/ Même que celle ci-dessus
☐ Not Applicable/ Ne s'applique pas

| Street Name/Nom de la rue SMALLER CITY STREET | Suite/Bureau 401 |

Street Name (cont'd)/Nom de la rue (suite)

City/Town/Ville
TORONTO   ONTARIO, CANADA

Postal Code/Code postal
M1M 1M1

7. Language of Preference
Langue préférée

English/Anglais [X]   French/Français ☐

8. Former Corporation Name if applicable/Raison sociale antérieure de la personne morale, le cas échéant.

☐ Not Applicable
Ne s'applique pas

| 9. Date commenced business activity in Ontario/ Date de début des activités en Ontario Year/Année Month/Mois Day/Jour 200- 04 15 | 10. Date ceased carrying on business activity in Ontario/ Date de cessation des activités en Ontario Year/Année Month/Mois Day/Jour ☐ Not Applicable/ Ne s'applique pas |

11. Jurisdiction of Incorporation/Amalgamation or Continuation. (Check appropriate box) Do not check more than one box.
Ressort de constitution/de fusion ou prorogation (cocher la case pertinente). Ne cocher qu'une seule case.

| 1. ☐ ALBERTA ALBERTA | 2. ☐ CANADA CANADA | 3. ☐ NEW BRUNSWICK NOUVEAU-BRUNSWICK | 4. ☐ NOVA SCOTIA NOUVELLE-ÉCOSSE | 5. ☐ QUEBEC QUÉBEC | 6. ☐ YUKON YUKON | 7. ☐ BRITISH COLUMBIA COLOMBIE-BRITANNIQUE |
| 8. ☐ MANITOBA MANITOBA | 9. ☐ NEWFOUNDLAND TERRE-NEUVE | 10. ☐ PRINCE EDWARD ISLAND ÎLE-DU-PRINCE-ÉDOUARD | 11. ☐ SASKATCHEWAN SASKATCHEWAN | 12. ☐ NORTHWEST TERRITORIES TERRITOIRES DU NORD-OUEST | 13. ☐ NUNAVUT NUNAVUT | |

If other please specify /
Si autre, veuillez préciser   STATE OF NEW YORK, USA

This information is being collected under the authority of The Corporations Information Act for the purpose of maintaining a public data base of corporate information. /
La Loi sur les renseignements exigés des personnes morales autorise la collecte de ces renseignements pour constituer une banque de données accessible au public.

FOR MINISTRY USE ONLY/À L'USAGE DU MINISTÈRE   ☐ See deficiency letter enclosed/Voir l'avis d'insuffisance ci-joint

07201 (02/2002)

FORM 2 - EXTRA PROVINCIAL CORPORATIONS/
FORMULE 2 - PERSONNES MORALES EXTRA-PROVINCIALES

Page 2/Page 2

Please type or print all information in block capital letters using black ink.
Prière de dactylographier les renseignements ou de les écrire en caractères d'imprimerie à l'encre noire.

FOR MINISTRY USE ONLY À L'USAGE DU MINISTÈRE SEULEMENT	Ontario Corporation Number/ Numéro matricule de la personne morale en Ontario	Date of Incorporation or Amalgamation Date de constitution ou fusion Year/Année Month/Mois Day/Jour	For Ministry Use Only À l'usage du ministère seulement
		200- 10 16	

12. Name and Office Address of the Chief Officer/Manager in Ontario/
Nom et adresse du bureau du directeur général/gérant en Ontario

☐ Not Applicable/Ne s'applique pas

Last Name/Nom de famille	First Name/Prénom	Middle Name/Autres prénoms
AGENT	ANDREW	WILLIAM

Street Number/Numéro civique
1500

Street Name/Nom de la rue
OFFICE ROAD

Street Name (cont'd)/Nom de la rue (suite)   Suite/Bureau

City/Town/Ville   Postal Code/Code postal
TORONTO   ONTARIO, CANADA   M2M 2M2

Date Effective Date d'entrée en vigueur   Year/Année Month/Mois Day/Jour   200- 04 15
Date Ceased Date de cessation des fonctions   Year/Année Month/Mois Day/Jour

13. Name and Office Address of Agent for Service in Ontario - Check One box
Nom et adresse du bureau du mandataire aux fins de signification en Ontario. Cocher la case pertinente.

[X] Not Applicable/Ne s'applique pas

Only applies to foreign business corporations
S'applique seulement aux personnes morales étrangères

a) ☐ Individual or   un particulier ou   b) ☐ Corporation   une personne morale
Complete appropriate sections below/Remplir les parties pertinentes ci-dessous.

a) Individual Name/Nom du particulier

Last Name/Nom de famille	First Name/Prénom	Middle Name/Autres prénoms

b) Ontario Corporation Number/Numéro matricule de la personne morale en Ontario

Corporation Name including punctuation/Raison sociale, y compris la ponctuation

c) Address/Adresse

c/o / a/s

Street No./N° civique   Street Name/Nom de la rue   Suite/Bureau

Street Name (cont'd)/Nom de la rue (suite)   City/Town/Ville

ONTARIO, CANADA   Postal Code/Code postal

14. (Print or type name in full of the person authorizing filing./ Dactylographier ou inscrire le prénom et le nom en caractères d'imprimerie de la personne qui autorise l'enregistrement.

Check appropriate box /
Cocher la case pertinente

I /
Je   IRVING B. SUCCESSFUL

certify that the information set out herein, is true and correct.
atteste que les renseignements précités sont véridiques et exacts.

D) [X] Director/Administrateur

O) ☐ Officer/Dirigeant

P) ☐ Other individual having knowledge of the affairs of the Corporation/Autre personne ayant connaissance des activités de la personne morale

NOTE/REMARQUE: Section 13 and 14 of the **Corporations Information Act** provide penalties for making false or misleading statements, or omissions.
Les articles 13 et 14 de la **Loi sur les renseignements exigés des personnes morales** prévoient des peines en cas de déclaration fausse ou trompeuse, ou d'omission.

This information is being collected under the authority of The Corporations Information Act for the purpose of maintaining a public data base of corporate information. /
La Loi sur les renseignements exigés des personnes morales autorise la collecte de ces renseignements pour constituer une banque de données accessible au public.

FOR MINISTRY USE ONLY/À L'USAGE DU MINISTÈRE   ☐ See deficiency letter enclosed/Voir l'avis d'insuffisance ci-joint

07201 (02/2002)

Ontario Corporation Number
Numéro de la compagnie en Ontario

APPLICATION FOR EXTRA-PROVINCIAL LICENCE/
DEMANDE EN VUE D'OBTENIR UN PERMIS EXTRAPROVINCIAL

1.

Form 1
Extra-
Provincial
Corporations
Act

Formule 1
*Loi de 1984
sur les
compagnies
extraprovinciales*

1. The name of the Corporation is (Print in UPPER CASE ONLY) :
   Dénomination sociale de la compagnie (Écrire en LETTRES MAJUSCULES SEULEMENT) :

| I | . | B | . | | O | U | T | S | I | D | E | R | | F | A | B | R | I | C | A | T | I | O | N | S | . | |
| L | T | D | . | | | | | | | | | | | | | | | | | | | | | | | | |

2. Business name or style, other than the corporate name, under which the corporation is to be licensed in Ontario, if any (if none, state so): / Nom, autre que la dénomination sociale, sous lequel un permis doit être délivré à la compagnie en Ontario, le cas échéant (si ce n'est pas le cas, veuillez l'indiquer) :

| N | O | N | E | | | | | | | | | | | | | | | | | | | | | | | | |

3. Jurisdiction to which subject:/
   Compétence législative :

STATE OF NEW YORK, USA
(Name of Province, State or Country) / (Province, État ou pays)

4. Date of incorporation/amalgamation:/
   Date de la constitution ou de la fusion :

| 200– | 10 | 16 |
| year / année | month / mois | day / jour |

5. Full address of the head or registered office: / Adresse du siège social :

SUITE 123 — 321 BIG CITY STREET
(Street & Number or R.R. Number & if Multi-Office Building give Room No.) / (Rue et numéro ou numéro de la R.R. et numéro du bureau)

NEW YORK
(Name of Municipality or Post Office) / (Municipalité ou bureau de poste)

012345
Postal/Zip Code / Code postal/zip

NEW YORK, USA
(Name of State or Country) / (État ou pays)

6. The corporation has been authorized to make this application by a resolution passed by the directors of the corporation at a meeting held on: / La compagnie est autorisée à présenter cette demande au moyen d'une résolution adoptée par ses administrateurs le :

| 200– | 01 | 10 |
| year / année | month / mois | day / jour |

07065(01/2002)

117

2.

7. Full address (including postal code) of the principal office or chief place of business in Ontario, if determined (if not, state so): / Adresse de l'établissement principal en Ontario, si elle est établie (si ce n'est pas le cas, l'indiquer) :

SUITE 410 — 104 SMALLER CITY STREET

(Street & Number or R.R. Number & if Multi-Office Building give Room No.) / (Rue et numéro ou numéro de la R.R. et numéro du bureau)

TORONTO

(Name of Municipality or Post Office) / (Municipalité ou bureau de poste)

M1M 1M1
Postal/Zip Code / Code postal/zip

8. Chief officer or manager in Ontario, if determined (if none, state so): /
   Premier dirigeant ou gérant en Ontario, s'il est désigné (si ce n'est pas le cas, l'indiquer) :

Name in full, including all first and middle names / Nom et prénoms	Residence address, giving Street & No. or R.R. No. & Municipality or Post Office and Postal Code: / Adresse personnelle y compris la rue et le numéro ou le numéro de la R.R., et le nom de la municipalité ou du bureau de poste et le code postal
ANDREW WILLIAM AGENT	1500 OFFICE ROAD TORONTO, ONTARIO M2M 2M2

9. The business which the corporation intends to carry on in Ontario is: /
   Les activités commerciales que la compagnie entend exercer en Ontario sont les suivantes :

3.

10. The corporate existence of the corporation is not limited in any way by statute or otherwise and the corporation is a valid and subsisting corporation. / La personnalité morale de la compagnie n'est restreinte d'aucune manière notamment par l'effet de la loi et la compagnie conserve sa validité et son existence juridique.

11. The corporation has the capacity to carry on business in Ontario. / La compagnie est habilitée à exercer ses activités commerciales en Ontario.

12. The corporation has the capacity to hold land without conditions or limitations. / La compagnie est habilitée à posséder des biens-fonds sans condition ni restriction.

13. The corporation hereby acknowledges that upon the licence being issued the corporation shall be subject to the provisions of the Extra-Provincial Corporations Act, the Corporations Information Act, the Corporations Tax Act and to such further and other legislative provisions as the Legislature of Ontario may deem expedient in order to secure the due management of the corporation's affairs and the protection of its creditors within Ontario. / La compagnie reconnaît par la présente que dès la délivrance du permis, elle sera assujettie aux dispositions de la *Loi sur les compagnies extraprovinciales*, de la Loi sur les renseignements exigés des compagnies et associations, de la *Loi sur l'imposition des personnes morales* ainsi qu'aux autres dispositions législatives ultérieures que la Législature de l'Ontario peut juger opportunes afin d'assurer la saine gestion des affaires de la compagnie et la protection de ses créanciers en Ontario.

This application is executed in duplicate. / La présente demande est signée en double exemplaire.

I.B. OUTSIDER FABRICATIONS LTD.
(Name of Corporation) / (Dénomination sociale de la compagnie)

By: / Signé : AWA
(Signature) / (Signature)

Director
(Description of Office) / (Fonctions)

(Corporate Seal) / (Sceau de la compagnie)

07065(01/2002)

119

SAMPLE 35
APPOINTMENT OF AGENT

Form 2
Extra-Provincial Corporations Act

Formule 2
Loi sur les personnes morales extraprovinciales

Check **(X)** the appropriate box
Cochez **(X)** la case appropriée

[X] APPOINTMENT OF AGENT FOR SERVICE
DÉSIGNATION DU MANDATAIRE AUX FINS DE SIGNIFICATION
or / ou

[ ] REVISED APPOINTMENT OF AGENT FOR SERVICE
MODIFICATION DE LA DÉSIGNATION DE MANDATAIRE

Ontario Corporation Number
Numéro de la société en Ontario   1.

___

I.B. OUTSIDER FABRICATIONS LTD.
(Name of appointing corporation) / *(Dénomination sociale de la société désignant le mandataire)*
(hereinafter called the "Corporation") hereby nominates, constitutes and appoints / (ci-après appelée la «société») constitue

ROBERT WILLIAM SMITH
(Name of agent giving first name, initials and surname; or full Corporate Name)
(Mandataire : prénom, initiale et nom de famille; ou dénomination sociale complète)

123 ATTORNEY ROAD, TORONTO, ONTARIO   M1M 3M3
(Business address of the agent, including Street Number, Suite or Room Number and Municipality)   Postal/Zip Code /
(Adresse d'affaires du mandataire : numéro et rue, bureau et municipalité)   *Code postal/zip*

its true and lawful agent for service, to act as such, and as such to sue and be sued, plead and be impleaded in any court in Ontario and generally on behalf of the corporation within Ontario to accept service of process and to receive all lawful notices and, for the purposes of the corporation, to do all acts and to execute all deeds and other instruments relating to the matters within the scope of this appointment. Until due lawful notice of the appointment of another and subsequent agent has been given to and accepted by the Director under the *Extra-Provincial Corporations Act*, service of process or of papers and notices upon the said agent for service shall be accepted by the corporation as sufficient service.

son mandataire aux fins de signification, qui agira en cette qualité, soutiendra à titre de demandeur ou de défendeur les actions en justice intentées en Ontario et, de manière générale, recevra et acceptera en Ontario, au nom de la société, tous actes de procédure et tous avis ou autorisés par la loi, accomplira toutes actions et signera tous actes et autres instruments relativement aux affaires entrant dans le cadre du présent mandat. Tant qu'un avis en bonne et due forme visant à désigner un autre mandataire n'aura pas été donné au directeur et accepté par lui, conformément à la Loi sur les personnes morales extraprovinciales, la société accepte comme suffisante la signification au mandataire susmentionné desdits actes de procédure, avis et autres documents.

Dated / *Date*   **200-**   **04**   **18**
year / *année*   month / *mois*   day / *jour*

I.B. OUTSIDER FABRICATIONS LTD.
(Name of Corporation / *Dénomination sociale de la société*)

BY:
PAR :   *I.B. Successful*   **PRESIDENT**
(Signature)   (Description of Office / *Titre*)

(Corporate Seal)
(Sceau de la société)   *Lotta Cash*   **TREASURER**
(Signature)   (Description of Office / *Titre*)

___

CONSENT TO ACT AS AGENT FOR SERVICE
CONSENTEMENT À AGIR EN QUALITÉ DE MANDATAIRE AUX FINS DE SIGNIFICATION

I
Je soussigné(e),   **ROBERT WILLIAM SMITH**
(Name of Agent in full; if Corporation, full Corporate Name)
(Nom complet du mandataire; si personne morale, dénomination sociale complète)

of
dont l'adresse d'affaires est :   **123 ATTORNEY ROAD, TORONTO, ONTARIO**
(Business address including Street Number, Suite or Room Number and Municipality)
(Adresse d'affaires : numéro et rue, numéro du bureau et municipalité)

Ontario, hereby consent to act as the agent for service in the Province of Ontario of
en Ontario, consens par les présentes à agir, dans la Province de l'Ontario, en qualité de mandataire aux fins de signification de

I.B. OUTSIDER FABRICATIONS LTD.
(Name of Corporation / *Dénomination sociale de la société*)

pursuant to the appointment executed by the said corporation on the
en vertu du présent mandat que ladite société a signé le

18TH day of / *jour de*   **APRIL**   , year / *année*   **200-**   ;

authorizing me to accept service of process and notices on its behalf
ledit mandat m'autorise à recevoir et à accepter au nom de la société tous actes de procédure, avis et autres documents.

Dated / *Date*   **200-**   **04**   **18**
year / *année*   month / *mois*   day / *jour*

I.M. Witness   *R.W. Smith*
(Signature of witness /   (Signature of the consenting person or Officer/Director of Corporation) /
Signature du témoin)   *(Signature du mandataire; si personne morale, signature du dirigeant/ administrateur agissant en son nom)*

07064(01/2002)

APPENDIX
DETAILED CHECKLIST OF STEPS TO BE FOLLOWED

1. Select three names for your corporation.

2. Call or write a private name search company to search your name.

3. Purchase package of forms.

4. Prepare articles and consents.

5. Forward the following documents to Companies Branch:

    (a) Duplicate originals of Articles

    (b) Consent forms, if applicable

    (c) Name search report

    (d) Cheque, certified, payable to the Minister of Finance for $360

6. Receive incorporation documents from CPPSB.

7. Order minute book and seal.

8. Complete Initial Return from the CPPSB.

9. Complete banking resolutions and open company bank account.

10. Prepare directors' and shareholders' resolutions.

11. Sign and file directors' and shareholders' resolutions in minute book along with issued signed share certificates and signed by-laws.

12. Complete registers in minute book.

13. Miscellaneous steps:

    (a) Draw up promissory notes for assets transferred to or loans made to the corporation in initial meetings.

    (b) Contact Retail Sales Department for exemption forms.

    (c) If motor vehicles are involved, visit the Motor Vehicle Branch for transfer forms.

14. File your Initial Return.